7 RIVALS

OF SUCCESS

CHRIS HARRIS

Dedication

The United States Military and Its Veterans

T his book is dedicated to every man and woman who has faithfully served in the United States military, especially my son, Stanton Harris. You are the true heroes of America, and I will always remain eternally grateful for your dedication, sacrifice, and courage. God bless and Godspeed to all the warriors who protect our great nation and diligently serve it with strength and honor.

Respectfully,

—*Chris Harris*

Table of Contents

Foreword

I had a chance meeting with Chris Harris several years ago, and he shared a copy of his book, "I Go Thru." It did not take long to recognize that Chris brings a unique set of life experiences and capabilities to his work. Because of that, he can offer compelling insights to help enhance our journey in today's challenging world.

In "7 Rivals of Success," he identifies key internal obstacles that can clutter our thinking and inhibit our path to success. Through straightforward and actionable recommendations, Chris provides a plan for overcoming the limitations that we sometimes impose upon ourselves.

As I reflect on my career and life path, I realize that there have been times when I allowed each of the 7 rivals to influence my direction and decisions unnecessarily. Hopefully, this book will serve as your secret weapon for neutralizing any rivals that may come your way.

—*Frank E. Borgsmiller / Retired Deloitte Consulting Partner*

Introduction

Every day, whether you know it or not, you're in fierce competition with seven rivals who are vying for your time, your energy, and your thoughts. From the moment the alarm goes off, the battle begins. Do you immediately get out of bed, or press the snooze button and go back to sleep? Do you eat a donut or something healthy? Do you catch up on emails and phone calls, or scroll through social media? Do you watch TV, or go for a walk? These unrelenting rivals are *fear, doubt, the past, idleness, adversity, distractions, and mindset.* Metaphorically, they are like hyenas: one-part natural predator, one-part scavenger, and one-part bully—collectively laughing as they gang up to steal your success and fulfillment.

Now for some good news—these rivals can be beaten! Throughout my lifetime, I have learned practical strategies for defeating them, which I share with you on the pages that follow. However, I didn't learn to reign victorious over these "thieves of achievement" by watching YouTube videos or documentaries, and my victories certainly didn't happen overnight. Instead, my success is the culmination of years of firsthand experience and hard-fought battles in the trenches of life, and I have the scars to prove it.

Here is a brief overview of where I learned the universal principles I share in this book:

I learned to "conquer fear" at 10 years old when my mother was sentenced to prison for being a drug addict and drug dealer. *Are you ready to break the chains of fear?*

I learned to "silence doubt" on my journey to the Martial Arts Hall of Fame, one punch at a time, one block at a time, and one belt at a time. *Are you ready to untie the lies?*

I learned to "let go of the past" once and for all when I knew I had to forgive countless people from my childhood before becoming a father. *Are you ready to let it go?*

I learned to "self-motivate through idleness" on my path to becoming number one in sales, where I had to prospect through rejection daily. *Are you ready to take action now?*

I learned to "overcome adversity" during my tumultuous childhood while in the foster care system and living homeless on the streets. *Are you ready to claim your power?*

I learned to "ignore distractions" when I was offered my first major book publishing deal and was given a non-negotiable deadline for its completion. *Are you ready to focus on growth?*

I learned to "transform my mindset" during the 25 years I trained elite warriors for the U.S. and its global allies as a private contractor. *Are you ready to shatter your limits?*

As a keynote speaker, I have addressed audiences from hundreds of companies and more than 60 countries, and I have found one thing to be true: every culture, regardless of income, education, age, or gender, faces these same seven rivals. The truths I share with you are universal, and their impact on your life can be profound if you are willing to put in the work and apply them.

If you are a leader, these principles will help you lead and inspire more effectively. If you are in sales, these principles will help you increase your or your team's sales performance. If you are facing life's challenges or are doing well but simply want more—these principles will provide a pathway to lasting success and fulfillment. And best of all—these rivals can be defeated using the tools you already possess!

—*Chris Harris / Author*

RIVAL 1

— ◆ —

F E A R

"Break the Chains"

Chapter One

Rational Fear Responds to Real Danger

Rival I: Fear

F ear is one of the most powerful forces in our lives. It can drive us to greatness or hold us captive in mediocrity. It can save our lives, but it can also sabotage our dreams. Fear is not inherently bad—it is necessary. But the key to mastering fear lies in understanding the difference between rational fear and irrational fear.

Rational fear is the guardian of our survival that responds to real danger. It warns us of real danger. It tells us to avoid walking too close to the edge of a cliff. It makes us cautious when driving in a storm. It sharpens our instincts and prepares us to act wisely when genuine risks arise. This fear is logical, reasonable, and necessary.

But then, there is irrational fear—the thief of potential, the enemy of progress. This is the fear that whispers lies in our ears. It tells us we are not good enough, not smart enough, not capable enough. It paralyzes us with self-doubt and convinces us that failure is not just possible but inevitable. It is the fear that stops us from taking the leap, speaking our minds, or stepping into the unknown.

Have you ever been afraid of failing? How many of you have hesitated to chase a dream because of the possibility of rejection? That, my friends, is irrational fear at work. It is not protecting you. It is deceiving you. It is keeping you locked in a prison of your own making.

But here's the truth—fear can be a liar. Fear magnifies risks and minimizes rewards. It makes mountains out of molehills and turns opportunities into obstacles. And the worst part? It convinces you it's doing you a favor. But you have a choice. You can let irrational fear rule your life, or you can rise above it.

So, how do we overcome irrational fear? First, we must recognize it for what it is. Ask yourself: Is this fear protecting me, or is it limiting me? Second, we must confront it. The only way to silence irrational fear is to challenge it with action. Fear hates movement. Every time you push through fear, you weaken its grip on you. Finally, we must reframe our mindset. Instead of fearing failure, see it as a stepping stone to success. Every great achiever in history has failed—many times. But they did not let fear define them. They pressed forward, learned, adapted, and triumphed.

Think about the influential leaders, the pioneers, the visionaries. They felt fear, just like you and me. But they did not bow to it. They stood in the face of their fears and moved forward anyway. And because of that, they changed the world.

What would your life look like if you refused to be ruled by irrational fear? What goals would you chase? What dreams would you resurrect? What risks would you take? Remember, fear will always be there. But courage is not the absence of fear—it is the decision that something else is more important. Choose courage. Choose to move forward. Choose to conquer fear.

Taking Action

Think | Write | Grow

Based on what you learned in this chapter:

What's something you will stop doing or a habit you will break?

_____

_____

What's something you will start doing or a habit you will create?

_____

_____

What's the potential positive impact of improving in this area?

_____

_____

Chapter Two

Intuition Whispers Prudent Advice

Rival I: Fear

L et's dive into one of the most powerful and underutilized gifts we all possess—intuition. That deep, inner knowing. That voice inside that whispers to us long before logic catches up. Some call it instinct, others call it a gut feeling, but whatever name you give it, intuition is one of the greatest tools for navigating life with confidence and purpose.

We live in a world that praises logic, analysis, and data. We are taught to seek proof, to demand evidence, to trust only what we can measure and quantify. And while reason has its place, there is another force within us that is just as powerful—our intuition. It is that immediate sense of understanding that comes without explanation. It is the feeling that tells you something is right or wrong before your mind has even had time to process it.

Think back to a time when you had a strong feeling about something—a situation, a person, or a decision. Maybe you ignored it, only to later regret that choice. Or maybe you followed it, and it led you exactly where you needed to be. That is the power of intuition. It is a guiding force that, when trusted, can shape our lives in extraordinary ways.

But why do so many of us ignore our intuition? Fear, doubt, and societal conditioning teach us to silence that inner voice. We second-guess ourselves. We look for external validation. We let the noise of the world drown out the wisdom within us. But deep down, we already know what we need to do. We just have to listen.

So, how do we strengthen and trust our intuition? First, we must learn to quiet the mind. In the chaos of daily life, our inner voice is often drowned out by distractions. Take time to slow down—through meditation, reflection, or even a simple walk in nature. The more we create space to listen, the clearer our intuition becomes.

Second, we must practice trusting ourselves. Every time we listen to our intuition and act on it, we strengthen that muscle. Start with small decisions—choosing what feels right instead of overthinking every possibility. Over time, this builds confidence in your ability to trust your own wisdom.

Third, we must separate fear from intuition. Fear is loud, anxious, and frantic. It is rooted in doubt and negativity. Intuition, on the other hand, is calm, clear, and steady. It does not shout—it simply knows. When making a decision, ask yourself: Am I feeling pressure and panic, or is this a quiet certainty? Learning to distinguish between the two is key to mastering intuition.

Great leaders, pioneers, and innovators throughout history have trusted their intuition. Steve Jobs once said, "Have the courage to follow your heart and intuition. They somehow already know what you truly want to become." Steve Jobs attributed much of his success to trusting his instincts. They, like so many others, understood that intuition is not irrational—it is deeply intelligent.

So, I ask: What is your intuition telling you? What have you been ignoring? What decisions are waiting to be made? Trust yourself. The answers you seek are already within you. Stop waiting for permission. Stop seeking approval. Stop letting fear talk you out of your destiny.

Your intuition is your compass. It will guide you toward the life you are meant to live. Trust it. Follow it. And watch as doors open, paths become clear, and your life transforms in ways you never imagined.

Taking Action

Think | Write | Grow

Based on what you learned in this chapter:

What's something you will stop doing or a habit you will break?

_____

_____

What's something you will start doing or a habit you will create?

_____

_____

What's the potential positive impact of improving in this area?

_____

_____

Chapter Three

Worry, Stress, and Pressure Can Motivate

Rival 1: Fear

W orry, stress, and pressure are three powerful forces that often carry a negative reputation. We are told to eliminate them, to avoid them at all costs. But what if I told you that these very things, the ones we often fear, can actually be the keys to unlocking our greatest potential?

Worry, stress, and pressure are not the enemies we think they are. They are signals, motivators, and even allies when harnessed correctly. They push us, challenge us, and force us to rise above obstacles. They are the weight that builds the muscle of resilience, the fire that forges strength, and the pressure that turns coal into diamonds.

Let's start with worry. Worry is often seen as wasted energy—spinning thoughts of 'what if' scenarios that may never happen. But what if we reframe it? What if, instead of seeing worry as a burden, we see it as a sign that something matters to us? Worry shows us where our priorities lie. It gives us insight into what we truly care about. Instead of letting worry paralyze us, we can use it as a guide, a tool to prepare and take action rather than sit in fear.

Now, let's talk about stress. Stress is a natural response to challenges. It sharpens our focus, increases our awareness, and helps us rise to the occasion. Think about athletes before a big game. They feel stress, but that stress is what makes them alert, agile, and ready to perform at their peak. The same applies to us in our daily lives. Stress, when managed correctly, can push us beyond our perceived limits. The key is not to let stress consume us, but to channel it into purposeful action. Stress reminds us that we are stepping outside our comfort zones, and that is where true growth happens.

And then, there's pressure. Pressure is often seen as overwhelming, something that crushes us. But pressure is what separates the great from the good. Pressure forces us to make decisions, to rise to the challenge, to prove to ourselves that we are capable of more than we ever imagined. Think about the most successful people in history—leaders, innovators, artists, and athletes. They all faced immense pressure, but instead of breaking under it, they thrived because of it. Pressure pushes us to show up, to perform, and to give our absolute best when it matters most.

So, how do we turn worry, stress, and pressure into motivation? First, we must acknowledge them, not fear them. These emotions are natural responses to ambition, responsibility, and growth. Second, we must shift our mindset. Instead of seeing them as obstacles, we must see them as fuel. We must reframe worry as preparation, stress as focus, and pressure as an opportunity to prove our strength. Finally, we must take action. Fear and doubt grow when we stand still, but they shrink when we move forward. The best way to conquer stress is through progress—one step at a time, one challenge at a time.

Think about this: What if every time you felt stressed, you saw it as proof that you were growing? What if every time you felt pressure, you saw it as an opportunity to show up and shine? What if every time you worried, you used it as motivation to prepare and take control?

Worry, stress, and pressure are not signs that you are weak. They are signs that you are alive, that you care, that you are pushing yourself toward something greater. Embrace them. Use them. Let them drive you forward. Because on the other side of stress is success, on the other side of worry is wisdom, and on the other side of pressure is greatness.

So, step into the challenge. Trust yourself. And turn every worry, every ounce of stress, and every moment of pressure into the fuel that propels you toward your dreams.

Taking Action

Think | Write | Grow

Based on what you learned in this chapter:

What's something you will stop doing or a habit you will break?

_____

_____

What's something you will start doing or a habit you will create?

_____

_____

What's the potential positive impact of improving in this area?

_____

_____

Chapter Four

Anxiety Ruminates the Exaggerated

Rival I: Fear

Anxiety is a silent force and a master of illusion. It takes a simple thought, an uncertainty, or a fear and magnifies it into something far greater than reality. It whispers worst-case scenarios into our minds, making us believe in dangers that do not exist. It makes us prisoners of our own imagination, caught in a cycle of overthinking, doubt, and hesitation.

Anxiety thrives on the imagined and the exaggerated. It turns a single mistake into the belief that we are failures. It takes one moment of discomfort and convinces us that disaster is inevitable. It makes the future look like a storm when, in reality, the skies may be clear. Anxiety is not reality—it is a distortion of it.

Think about this: How many times have you worried endlessly about something that never actually happened? How many nights have you lost sleep over an outcome that turned out to be far less catastrophic than you feared? That is anxiety at work. It creates scenarios in our minds that are bigger, scarier, and more consuming than the truth. And the more we feed these thoughts, the stronger they become.

But here's what you must remember—you are not your anxious thoughts. You are not the stories your mind tells you in moments of fear. Anxiety may paint pictures of failure, rejection, or uncertainty, but those pictures are not real. They are just shadows of what could be, not reflections of what is.

So, how do we break free from anxiety's grip? First, we must recognize it for what it is—an exaggeration, not a truth. When an anxious thought arises, challenge it. Ask yourself: Is this real, or is my mind magnifying a possibility? Second, we must shift our focus. Instead of dwelling on fear, we must ground ourselves in the present. Anxiety lives in the 'what ifs' of tomorrow, but peace is found in the 'what is' of today. Practicing mindfulness, deep breathing, and gratitude can help bring us back to reality.

Third, we must take action. Anxiety thrives in inaction. The longer we sit with fearful thoughts, the stronger they become. But when we move forward despite our fears, we weaken anxiety's hold on us. Courage is not the absence of anxiety—it is the decision to keep going despite it. Every step you take through fear is proof that you are stronger than the thoughts that try to hold you back.

Finally, remember this: You have faced anxiety before, and you have overcome it. The worries of yesterday did not break you, and the fears of today will not define you. You are capable of more than your anxious mind tells you. You have the power to rise above the exaggerated and step into the truth.

So, the next time anxiety tries to convince you that you are not enough, that failure is certain, or that the worst will happen—pause. Take a deep breath. Remind yourself that these are just thoughts. They do not control me. I choose to see reality, not the illusion anxiety creates.

You are stronger than your fears. You are braver than your doubts. And you are capable of a life beyond anxiety's grasp. Believe it, live it, and shatter the limits of your past.

Taking Action

Think | Write | Grow

Based on what you learned in this chapter:

What's something you will stop doing or a habit you will break?

_____

_____

What's something you will start doing or a habit you will create?

_____

_____

What's the potential positive impact of improving in this area?

_____

_____

Chapter Five

Phobias Are Common and Treatable

Rival I: Fear

F ear is one of the most basic and universal human emotions. It keeps us alert, protects us from danger, and helps us survive. But sometimes, fear grows beyond its purpose. It becomes overwhelming, irrational, and paralyzing. This is what we call a phobia—a fear that takes control, limits our actions, and holds us back from living fully. It's important to remember that phobias are common and, more importantly, they are treatable.

If you have ever felt an intense fear of something—whether it's heights, flying, public speaking, spiders, or enclosed spaces—you are not alone. Phobias affect millions of people around the world, regardless of age, background, or experience. Some of the most confident and successful individuals have battled their own fears. The difference between those who remain trapped by them and those who break free is the belief that overcoming fear is possible.

Many people believe that their phobias define them and that they are destined to live in fear forever. But this is simply not true. Phobias are learned responses, and just as they were learned, they can be unlearned. Science and psychology have proven time and again that fear can be rewired, that new associations can be built, and that courage is not something we are born with—it is something we develop.

So, how do we overcome phobias? First, we must acknowledge them. Many people avoid their fears, hoping they will disappear on their own. But avoidance only makes fear stronger. The more we run from fear, the more power we give it. The first step to overcoming a phobia is to face it with awareness and understanding.

Second, we must take gradual steps. Fear cannot be erased overnight, but it can be chipped away little by little. This is called exposure therapy—facing your fear in small, manageable steps until it no longer holds the same power over you. If you are afraid of public speaking, start by speaking in front of one person, then a small group, and then a larger audience. If you are afraid of heights, take one step higher each time until your mind learns that there is no real danger. Progress may be slow, but every step forward is a victory.

Third, we must reframe our thinking. Phobias thrive on exaggeration. Our minds create worst-case scenarios that are unlikely to happen. But what if we changed the story? What if, instead of imagining failure, embarrassment, or disaster, we imagined success, growth, and triumph? Fear is a mental game, and the way we think about it determines how much power it has over us.

And finally, we must seek support. No one should battle fear alone. Whether it's through therapy, coaching, or simply talking to a friend, sharing our fears reduces their weight. There is strength in admitting vulnerability, and there is courage in seeking help. Many people have conquered their phobias, and so can you.

Imagine a life where fear no longer dictates your choices. Imagine feeling confident in situations that once made you panic. Imagine turning your fear into fuel for growth. That life is possible. It is not reserved for a lucky few—it is available to anyone willing to take the steps toward freedom.

So, I challenge you to face your fears, even in small ways. Take that first step. Do not let phobias define you, because they do not have to. You are stronger than you think, braver than you believe, and more capable than you imagine. Fear may be common, but so is the ability to overcome it. Choose courage and watch your life transform.

Taking Action

Think | Write | Grow

Based on what you learned in this chapter:

What's something you will stop doing or a habit you will break?

_____

_____

What's something you will start doing or a habit you will create?

_____

_____

What's the potential positive impact of improving in this area?

_____

_____

Chapter Six

Awareness Reduces Emotional Triggers

Rival 1: Fear

Emotions are powerful. They can inspire us, guide us, and connect us to others. But they can also overwhelm us, cloud our judgment, and lead us to react in ways we later regret. We all have emotional triggers—moments when a word, a situation, or an event sets off an intense reaction within us. But what if I told you that you have the power to reduce these triggers? That the key to emotional control lies in one simple, yet profound skill—awareness.

Awareness is the ability to observe your emotions without being controlled by them. It is the space between stimulus and response. It is the difference between reacting impulsively and responding thoughtfully. When we become aware of our emotional triggers, we regain control over our minds, our actions, and ultimately, our lives.

Think about the last time you were triggered. Maybe someone criticized you, and you instantly felt defensive. Maybe a past memory surfaced, and suddenly you were consumed by anger or sadness. These reactions often feel automatic, as if we have no choice but to feel the way we do. But the truth is, we do have a choice. When we become aware of what triggers us and why, we can change our responses. We can shift from being controlled by emotions to mastering them.

So, how do we cultivate awareness and reduce emotional triggers? First, we must learn to pause. In moments of emotional intensity, take a breath. Before reacting, give yourself space to observe what's happening inside you. Ask yourself: What am I feeling? Why am I feeling this way? What story am I telling myself about this situation? That pause alone can change everything. It allows logic to step in before emotions take over.

Second, we must identify our patterns. Emotional triggers are often rooted in past experiences, unhealed wounds, or deeply held beliefs. If certain situations or words repeatedly cause the same emotional reaction, it is a sign that there is something deeper to explore. Awareness allows us to recognize these patterns, understand their origins, and begin the healing process.

Third, we must shift our perspective. Many times, our emotional reactions come not from the situation itself, but from the meaning we assign to it. A comment from a coworker may trigger feelings of inadequacy—not because the comment was truly hurtful, but because, deep down, we doubt ourselves. When we become aware of our internal narratives, we can challenge them. Instead of assuming the worst, we can choose a new, empowering perspective.

Finally, we must practice self-compassion. Emotional awareness is not about suppressing emotions or judging ourselves for having them. It is about understanding them with kindness. When you feel triggered, remind yourself: I am human. I am learning. I have the power to change. Self-awareness is not about perfection—it is about growth.

The greatest leaders, the most successful individuals, and the happiest people all have one thing in common—they understand their emotions rather than being ruled by them. They do not let triggers dictate their actions. They use awareness as a tool for emotional freedom.

So, I ask: What triggers you? What emotions tend to control you? And how can you become more aware of them? The moment you begin to observe your emotions rather than being consumed by them, you reclaim your power. You are no longer a victim of your reactions—you are the master of them.

Awareness is the path to emotional strength. It is the key to peace, resilience, and wisdom. It is within you right now, waiting to be used. So choose awareness. Choose growth. And choose well-being.

Taking Action

Think | Write | Grow

Based on what you learned in this chapter:

What's something you will stop doing or a habit you will break?

_____

_____

What's something you will start doing or a habit you will create?

_____

_____

What's the potential positive impact of improving in this area?

_____

_____

Chapter Seven

Courage Requires Doing Things Afraid

Rival I: Fear

C ourage is not the absence of fear. Courage is taking action despite fear. It is standing up, stepping forward, and moving through uncertainty even when doubt whispers in your ear. We often wait for fear to disappear before we take a leap, before we start something new, before we face our biggest challenges. But the truth is, if we wait for fear to leave, we may never move at all.

Every significant achievement in history was accomplished by someone who felt fear—but acted anyway. The leaders who changed the world, the athletes who broke records, the pioneers who dared to go beyond the limits of what was thought possible—they all had fear. But they refused to let fear stop them. Instead, they walked forward, fear and all, because they knew that courage is not about feeling ready. It's about doing it afraid.

Think about the moments in your own life when fear tried to hold you back. Maybe it was the fear of failure, the fear of rejection, or the fear of the unknown. Maybe it was fear of what others might think, or fear that you weren't good enough. Fear has many disguises, and it speaks loudly. But here's the secret—fear only has power if you listen to it. The moment you decide to move forward despite fear, you take its power away.

So, how do we build courage? How do we train ourselves to do things afraid? First, we must change our mindset. Fear is not a stop sign—it's a signal that you are stepping into growth. The presence of fear means you are stretching beyond your comfort zone, and that is where true transformation happens. When fear arises, don't retreat—recognize it as proof that you are about to do something meaningful.

Second, we must take small steps. Courage is not always about giant leaps. It is often about taking one small step forward, then another, and another. If speaking in public terrifies you, start by speaking in front of a friend. If starting a business feels overwhelming, take the first small action today. Each step you take while afraid weakens fear's grip and strengthens your confidence.

Third, we must embrace failure as part of the journey. Many times, fear is rooted in the idea that we might fail. But failure is not the opposite of success—it is a stepping stone to it. Every successful person has faced setbacks, rejections, and obstacles. The difference is that they kept moving forward, learning from each challenge, and refusing to let fear win.

And finally, we must remember why we started. Fear loves to make us forget our purpose, our dreams, and our potential. But when we keep our focus on our goal—on the impact we want to make, on the life we want to create—fear becomes smaller. Your mission, your passion, and your dreams are bigger than your fear. Hold on to that truth.

So, I challenge you: Do it afraid. Make the call. Take the first step. Speak up. Show up. Don't let fear decide your future. The life you want, the success you seek, and the person you are meant to become are all on the other side of fear. And the only way to get there is to step forward—courageously, boldly, and yes, even afraid.

Because courage isn't waiting for fear to go away. Courage is moving forward despite it.

Taking Action

Think | Write | Grow

Based on what you learned in this chapter:

What's something you will stop doing or a habit you will break?

_____

_____

What's something you will start doing or a habit you will create?

_____

_____

What's the potential positive impact of improving in this area?

_____

_____

RIVAL 2

---◆---

D O U B T

"Untie the Lies"

Chapter Eight

Energy Can Neither Be Created nor Destroyed

Rival 2: Doubt

The statement "energy can neither be created nor destroyed" is a fundamental principle in physics known as the law of conservation of energy, which states that energy can only be transformed from one form to another. Not only is this a law of physics, but it is also one of the greatest truths about life itself. Everything we experience—our thoughts, our emotions, our struggles, our triumphs—is energy in motion. The question is not whether we have energy, but how we choose to use it.

Every challenge, every obstacle, every doubt that you have ever faced carries energy. Fear is energy. So are frustration, stress, and pain. But here's the incredible truth: You have the power to take that energy and transform it into something greater. You can take your struggles and turn them into strength. You can take your fears and convert them into courage. You can take every ounce of doubt and use it as fuel to push forward.

Think about the moments in life when you felt stuck, exhausted, or defeated. It wasn't because you lacked energy—it was because your energy was trapped in negative emotions or limiting beliefs. The key to success, to happiness, to fulfillment, is learning how to shift that energy into action, growth, and resilience.

How do we do that? How do we transform our energy into something powerful?

First, we must recognize where our energy is going. Are you spending your energy worrying about things you cannot control? Are you pouring your energy into fear rather than faith? Are you letting negative experiences drain you instead of using them to build you? Awareness is the first step to transformation.

Second, we must redirect our energy with intention. Instead of dwelling on failure, use that energy to learn, to improve, to rise. Instead of letting stress break you, channel it into focus, discipline, and determination. The greatest achievers in history did not avoid struggle—they harnessed it. They turned their hardships into stepping stones. They transformed pain into purpose.

Third, we must fuel ourselves with the right energy. Just as we cannot run a car on the wrong type of fuel, we cannot run our lives on negativity, doubt, or fear. Surround yourself with people who uplift you. Fill your mind with thoughts that inspire you. Take care of your body, your mind, and your soul, because the energy you put in determines the energy you get out.

And finally, we must remember that energy is limitless. There is no cap on your potential. There is no limit to how much you can grow, achieve, and impact the world. The energy you need to succeed, to transform, to thrive—it is already within you. You don't need to create it—you just need to direct it.

So, I challenge you: Take the energy that fear has given you and turn it into courage. Take the energy that failure has given you and turn it into wisdom. Take the energy that pain has given you and turn it into power. You are not weak. You are not lacking. You are full of energy waiting to be transformed.

Energy cannot be created or destroyed—but it can be used to create the life you've always imagined.

Taking Action

Think | Write | Grow

Based on what you learned in this chapter:

What's something you will stop doing or a habit you will break?

_____

_____

What's something you will start doing or a habit you will create?

_____

_____

What's the potential positive impact of improving in this area?

_____

_____

Chapter Nine

The Wolf That Is Fed the Most Will Win

Rival 2: Doubt

There is an old Cherokee story that teaches us a powerful lesson about life. A grandfather tells his grandson, "Inside every person, there are two wolves in a constant battle. One wolf represents fear, doubt, anger, jealousy, and negativity. The other wolf represents courage, strength, love, kindness, and resilience."

The grandson, curious, asks, "Which wolf will win?"

The grandfather replies, "The one you feed."

Every single day, we make a choice about which wolf to feed. We decide whether to give our energy to doubt or to determination, to negativity or to possibility, to fear or to faith. The wolf that grows stronger is the one we nourish, the one we focus on, the one we allow to guide us.

So, I ask you: Which wolf are you feeding?

We all experience moments of fear, frustration, and self-doubt. It is natural. The negative wolf whispers to us that we are not good enough, that we will fail, that we should give up. But just because the voice exists does not mean we must listen. Just because the negative wolf is there does not mean we must feed it.

Instead, we can make the conscious decision to feed the wolf of strength and perseverance. We can choose to focus on solutions rather than problems. We can choose to see obstacles as opportunities to grow. We can choose to speak words of encouragement rather than words of defeat.

How do we do this? How do we ensure that the right wolf wins?

First, we must control our thoughts. Our minds are powerful, and what we think about, we bring about. If we constantly tell ourselves we are not capable, we will act accordingly. But if we fill our minds with thoughts of confidence, resilience, and belief, we will rise to meet any challenge. Train your mind to feed the right wolf.

Second, we must watch the words we speak. Words shape reality. When we say, "I can't," we feed the negative wolf. When we say, "I will find a way," we feed the wolf of strength. Speak life into your dreams. Speak power into your actions. Speak victory into your challenges.

Third, we must take action. Thoughts and words are powerful, but they must be followed by action. Feed the right wolf through your decisions. Face your fears instead of running from them. Push forward when it would be easier to quit. Keep going when doubt creeps in. Every time you take action in the face of adversity, you starve the negative wolf and strengthen the positive one.

Finally, we must surround ourselves with the right energy. The people we associate with, the content we consume, the habits we build—all of these things determine which wolf thrives. Choose to be around those who uplift you. Choose to fill your mind with inspiration and knowledge. Choose habits that align with growth and success.

The battle between the two wolves never ends. It is fought in our minds, our hearts, and our daily choices. But the outcome is always within our control. The wolf of fear, doubt, and negativity will only win if we allow it to. But if we consciously, intentionally, and consistently feed the wolf of courage, strength, and resilience, that is the wolf that will lead us.

So, I challenge you: Be mindful of what you feed. Be intentional about your thoughts, your words, your actions, and your environment. Choose to nourish the wolf that will take you toward your dreams. Because in the end, the wolf you feed the most is the one that will win.

Taking Action

Think | Write | Grow

Based on what you learned in this chapter:

What's something you will stop doing or a habit you will break?

_____

_____

What's something you will start doing or a habit you will create?

_____

_____

What's the potential positive impact of improving in this area?

_____

_____

Chapter Ten

Optimism Is a Powerful Force Multiplier

Rival 2: Doubt

O ptimism is not just a positive attitude—it is a force that shapes our reality. It is the belief that, no matter what challenges come our way, there is always a way forward. Life is filled with ups and downs, victories and setbacks, joy, and struggles. But the people who rise above, who succeed, who live fulfilling lives, are not those who never face hardship. They are those who choose to see possibility where others see defeat.

Optimism is not about ignoring difficulties or pretending that problems do not exist. It is about choosing to focus on solutions instead of obstacles, on opportunities instead of limitations. It is about understanding that setbacks are temporary, that failure is just a stepping stone to success, and that even in our darkest moments, there is a reason to hope.

Optimism fuels resilience, and resilience leads to breakthroughs. So, how do we cultivate optimism in our daily lives? How do we train our minds to see the good when circumstances seem difficult?

First, we must take control of our thoughts. The mind is like a garden—what we plant is what grows. If we constantly feed it with negativity, doubt, and fear, those emotions will take over. But if we plant seeds of hope, confidence, and possibility, we will cultivate a mindset that is strong and unshakable. When faced with a challenge, ask yourself: What can I learn from this? How can I grow? How can I turn this into an opportunity?

Second, we must shift our focus. Optimism is a choice. Instead of dwelling on what went wrong, focus on what can go right. Instead of fixating on what you don't have, appreciate what you do have. Train your mind to see possibilities, even in difficult situations. When you make this shift, you find that solutions appear where you once saw only problems.

Third, we must take action. Optimism is not just about thinking positively—it is about acting with purpose. It is about stepping forward, even when the path is uncertain. It is about believing in your ability to adapt, to learn, and to overcome. Every action you take toward your goals weakens fear and strengthens belief. When you act despite doubt, you prove to yourself that challenges do not define you—your response to them does.

Fourth, we must surround ourselves with the right energy. The people we spend time with, the conversations we engage in, and the messages we absorb shape our perspectives. Negativity is contagious, but so is optimism. Choose to be around those who lift you up, who inspire you, and who believe in possibilities. Surround yourself with books, music, and content that fuels your spirit rather than drains it.

And finally, we must practice gratitude. Gratitude is the foundation of optimism. When we focus on what we already have, rather than what we lack, we shift our mindset from scarcity to abundance. Even in our toughest times, there is always something to be grateful for. Gratitude rewires our brains to seek the good, and the more we look for it, the more we will find.

So, I ask you: What are you choosing to see? Are you focusing on limitations, or are you embracing possibilities? The power of optimism is not reserved for a lucky few—it is available to all of us. It is a habit, a mindset, and a way of living that can be cultivated every single day.

Life will not always be easy. Challenges will come. But with optimism, you will always find a way through. You will rise above. You will turn obstacles into opportunities and setbacks into stepping stones. Choose to believe in yourself and your future, and in the endless possibilities that lie ahead.

Taking Action

Think | Write | Grow

Based on what you learned in this chapter:

What's something you will stop doing or a habit you will break?

_____

_____

What's something you will start doing or a habit you will create?

_____

_____

What's the potential positive impact of improving in this area?

_____

_____

Chapter Eleven

Gratitude Subdues Fear and Negativity

Rival 2: Doubt

There is one simple, yet powerful force that can change the way we see the world, the way we respond to challenges, and the way we move through life. That force is gratitude.

Gratitude is more than just saying "thank you." It is a mindset, a way of seeing the world, a choice to focus on what we have rather than what we lack. And perhaps most importantly, gratitude is the antidote to fear and negativity. It has the power to shift our focus from worry to appreciation, from doubt to confidence, from frustration to peace.

Fear thrives in the unknown. It feeds on uncertainty, making us believe the worst is yet to come. Negativity is its closest companion, magnifying our problems, making obstacles seem insurmountable. But gratitude disrupts this pattern. Gratitude reminds us of what is good, what is possible, and what is already working in our lives. It forces us to see the light, even when darkness threatens to take over.

Think about a time when fear held you back. Maybe it was fear of failure, fear of rejection, or fear of the future. In that moment, your focus was likely on what could go wrong. But what if, instead of focusing on what was missing, you focused on what you already have? What if, instead of fearing failure, you were grateful for the opportunity to try? What if, instead of dreading the unknown, you appreciated the lessons you have already learned? Fear loses its grip when gratitude takes its place.

Negativity, too, struggles to survive in the presence of gratitude. It is impossible to feel angry and grateful at the same time. It is impossible to dwell on problems while actively appreciating the good in your life. The moment you start counting your blessings, negativity begins to fade.

So, how do we cultivate gratitude and use it to overcome fear and negativity?

First, we must make gratitude a daily practice. Start each day by recognizing at least three things you are grateful for. They don't have to be big—sometimes the smallest things bring the greatest joy. A warm cup of coffee, a kind word from a friend, the simple fact that you have another day to live and grow. When we train our minds to seek the good, we begin to find it everywhere.

Second, we must reframe challenges with gratitude. Instead of seeing obstacles as setbacks, see them as opportunities to grow. Instead of fearing failure, be grateful for the chance to learn. Every difficult moment carries a lesson, and every challenge strengthens us in some way. When we choose gratitude, we turn struggles into stepping-stones.

Third, we must express gratitude to others. Gratitude is not just about what we feel—it is about what we share. Tell people how much you appreciate them. A simple "thank you" can brighten someone's day and create a ripple effect of positivity. When we lift others up, we lift ourselves up as well.

And finally, we must let gratitude guide our thoughts. When fear creeps in, replace it with appreciation. When negativity arises, counter it with thankfulness. Gratitude is a habit, and like any habit, it grows stronger with practice.

So, I challenge you: Choose gratitude. Choose to focus on what is good. Choose to see the blessings, even in difficult times. Because when you fill your heart with gratitude, fear has no place to stay. When you embrace appreciation, negativity has no room to grow. Remember that gratitude is not just a feeling—it is a power.

Taking Action

Think | Write | Grow

Based on what you learned in this chapter:

What's something you will stop doing or a habit you will break?

_____

_____

What's something you will start doing or a habit you will create?

_____

_____

What's the potential positive impact of improving in this area?

_____

_____

Chapter Twelve

A Positive Environment Cultivates Positivity

Rival 2: Doubt

W e are shaped by the environments we create and the energy we surround ourselves with. Our mindset, our emotions, and even our success are deeply influenced by the people, places, and habits that make up our daily lives. A positive environment doesn't just happen—it is built with intention, and when cultivated, it fuels positivity, well-being, and personal growth.

Imagine waking up every day in a space that energizes you, surrounded by people who uplift and inspire you. Imagine working in an atmosphere where encouragement replaces criticism, where kindness outweighs negativity, and where every challenge is met with a mindset of possibility rather than defeat. This kind of environment is not a luxury—it is a necessity for those who want to thrive.

Positivity is not just a feeling—it is a product of the energy we absorb. Just as a plant flourishes in the right soil, water, and sunlight, we, too, thrive in the right environment. When we intentionally shape our surroundings, we influence our thoughts, our actions, and ultimately, our future.

So, how do we create and maintain a positive environment?

First, we must be mindful of the people we surround ourselves with. Energy is contagious. If you are constantly around negativity, doubt, and criticism, it will drain your spirit. But when you are around those who encourage, uplift, and inspire, you naturally become more positive and motivated. Choose to spend time with people who challenge you to grow, who believe in your potential, and who remind you of the good in life.

Second, we must cultivate positive habits. A healthy environment isn't just about who is around us—it's about what we do daily. Small habits like expressing gratitude, engaging in uplifting conversations, consuming inspiring content, and practicing kindness can transform our outlook. When we feed ourselves positivity, we strengthen our ability to stay optimistic and resilient.

Third, we must design our physical space for well-being. Our surroundings affect our mood and productivity more than we realize. A cluttered, dark, or uninspiring space can drain our energy, while an organized, bright, and inviting space can boost our motivation and creativity. Take control of your surroundings—whether it's your home, workplace, or even the digital spaces you engage with. Create an environment that supports your goals and makes you feel inspired every day.

Fourth, we must protect our energy. Not everything deserves our attention. Drama, gossip, and negativity will always exist, but we have the power to tune them out. Be mindful of what you consume—whether it's the news, social media, or conversations. If something consistently drains your energy, distance yourself from it. Your peace of mind is invaluable and must be protected.

And finally, we must be a source of positivity for others. The best way to cultivate a positive environment is to be the example of what we wish to see. When we radiate kindness, encouragement, and optimism, we attract the same energy in return. Be the person who lifts others up, who sees potential where others see obstacles, and who spreads hope and encouragement in difficult times.

Creating a positive environment is a choice that leads to better well-being, stronger relationships, and greater success. When we take control of the energy we allow into our lives, we become unstoppable. Choose to build an environment that reflects the life you want to live and where positivity flourishes.

Taking Action

Think | Write | Grow

Based on what you learned in this chapter:

What's something you will stop doing or a habit you will break?

_____

_____

What's something you will start doing or a habit you will create?

_____

_____

What's the potential positive impact of improving in this area?

_____

_____

Chapter Thirteen

Finding Solutions Beats Finding Faults

Rival 2: Doubt

I n life, we are constantly faced with two choices, which are to dwell on problems or seek solutions. Every challenge, obstacle, and setback presents us with an opportunity to either focus on what went wrong or figure out how to make things right. And the truth is, the people who succeed, the people who grow, the people who make a difference, are the ones who choose to focus on solutions rather than faults.

It is easy to point out what is wrong. Blaming, complaining, or criticizing takes no effort. Fault-finding is reactive—it looks backward, searching for who or what to blame. But solution-seeking is proactive—it looks forward, searching for ways to improve, grow, move beyond the problem, and create something better.

So, how do we train ourselves to become solution-seekers instead of fault-finders?

First, we must shift our mindset. When challenges arise, pause instead of immediately reacting with frustration and ask yourself, "What can be done?" The power of your mind is incredible, and when you train it to seek solutions rather than blame, you start seeing possibilities where others see dead ends. Problems are not stop signs but guidelines that point us toward solutions.

Second, we must take responsibility, as blame gets us nowhere. The moment we stop blaming others, the economy, our circumstances, or even ourselves, and instead take ownership of the situation, we gain the power to change it. Responsibility is not about pointing fingers at others but about taking control of our future.

Third, we must embrace a problem-solving attitude. Every time you encounter an obstacle, break it down. Ask yourself: What is the real issue? What options do I have? What is the first step I can take right now? Solutions come to those who actively look for them. If you train yourself to approach every problem with curiosity rather than frustration, you will find that most challenges have an answer waiting to be discovered.

Fourth, we must surround ourselves with solution-oriented people. Negativity is contagious, but so is optimism. If you are surrounded by people who constantly complain, blame, and focus on faults, it will be harder to develop a problem-solving mindset. But if you surround yourself with people who focus on progress, look for ways forward, and inspire you to think bigger, you will also develop that mindset.

Finally, we must take action. Finding solutions is not just about thinking—it is about doing. The best ideas in the world mean nothing without execution. Small steps lead to big changes. Every time you take action toward a solution, you prove to yourself that problems do not define you—your response to them does.

So, I challenge you to be a solution-seeker. The next time you face a problem, resist the urge to dwell on what went wrong. Instead, focus on what can be done. Choose to create rather than criticize. Choose to build rather than blame. Choose to move forward rather than remain stuck.

Because in the end, success belongs to those who see beyond problems and into possibilities. Your future is shaped not by the challenges you face, but by the solutions you choose to create.

Taking Action

Think | Write | Grow

Based on what you learned in this chapter:

What's something you will stop doing or a habit you will break?

_____

_____

What's something you will start doing or a habit you will create?

_____

_____

What's the potential positive impact of improving in this area?

_____

_____

Chapter Fourteen

Fall Down Seven Times, Get Up Eight

Rival 2: Doubt

L ife is not about how many times you fall—it is about how many times you rise. The path to success is not smooth, not easy, and certainly not free of setbacks. But those who win, those who achieve, those who make a difference, are not the ones who never fall. They are the ones who refuse to stay down.

There is a powerful Japanese proverb that says, "Fall seven times, get up eight." It is a simple phrase, yet it holds the essence of resilience, perseverance, and the unbreakable spirit of a winner. No matter how many times life knocks you down, you must get back up. Because every fall is not the end of the road—it is just part of the journey.

Think about the greatest athletes, the most successful entrepreneurs, the pioneers, the visionaries. They all have something in common, which is failure. They have faced rejection, disappointment, and moments where everything seemed to fall apart. But instead of giving up, they stood back up, adjusted their strategy, and kept moving forward. Because they understood that failure is not a final destination—it is just a stepping stone to success.

So, how do we develop this unshakable resilience? How do we train ourselves to get back up every time life pushes us down?

First, we must change our mindset about failure. Failure is not a reflection of weakness—it is proof that you are trying, growing, and pushing beyond your comfort zone. Every fall is an opportunity to learn. Instead of asking, "Why did this happen to me?" ask, "What can I learn from this?" Winners see setbacks not as defeats but as lessons.

Second, we must embrace perseverance. The difference between those who succeed and those who give up is persistence. Talent alone does not create champions—grit does. Hard work does. The willingness to keep going when everything inside you says to quit. When you fall, remind yourself: This is not the end. This is just another chance to prove how strong I am.

Third, we must develop emotional resilience. Falling hurts. Failing is disappointing. But pain is temporary—quitting lasts forever. True strength is built in the moments when you choose to stand up despite the pain, despite the doubt, despite the setbacks. Train yourself to see struggle as part of the process, not as a reason to stop.

Fourth, we must surround ourselves with the right people. The journey is tough, but you don't have to do it alone. Winners build support systems—mentors, friends, family—who remind them of their strength when they forget. Surround yourself with people who lift you up, who push you to be better, who remind you that falling is just part of the climb.

And finally, we must take action. The only way to rise after a fall is to stand up and move forward. Action creates momentum. Even if you have to start small, start now. Keep pushing, keep striving, keep going. Because every step forward brings you closer to your goal.

So, I ask you: Are you willing to get back up? Are you willing to keep fighting, to keep believing, to keep rising every time life knocks you down? Because if you are, then nothing can stop you.

Fall seven times, get up eight. That is the mindset of a winner. That is the heart of a champion. And that is the key to turning every setback into a comeback.

Taking Action

Think | Write | Grow

Based on what you learned in this chapter:

What's something you will stop doing or a habit you will break?

_____

_____

What's something you will start doing or a habit you will create?

_____

_____

What's the potential positive impact of improving in this area?

_____

_____

RIVAL 3

❖

T H E   P A S T

"Let It Go"

Chapter Fifteen

No One Owes Me Anything

Rival 3: The Past

There is a hard truth that many struggle to accept, but it is one of the most liberating truths you will ever hear: Nobody owes you anything, and nobody is coming to rescue you. It may sound harsh, but it is the reality. And once you embrace it, you gain the most powerful thing of all—control over your own life. The moment you stop waiting for someone to save you, for circumstances to change, or for luck to suddenly fall in your favor, you step into your true power. Because success, happiness, and fulfillment are not given to you—they are earned.

Too many people spend their lives waiting. Waiting for someone to recognize their potential. Waiting for the perfect opportunity. Waiting for life to be fair. But waiting is not a proactive strategy. Waiting does not lead to growth. The truth is, life is not fair. Nobody is obligated to hand you success. If you want something, you have to go get it. If you want change, you have to make it happen. If you want more, you must be willing to do more.

Think about the people who have achieved greatness. They did not sit around hoping someone would come along and fix their problems. They did not expect the world to hand them success. They took ownership of their lives. They put in the work. They failed, learned, adapted, and kept pushing forward. And that is exactly what you must do.

So, how do we embrace this mindset and take full responsibility for our lives?

First, stop blaming others. It is easy to point fingers at circumstances, at people, at the system. But blame gives away your power. The moment you accept full responsibility for where you are, you gain the power to change it. It is not about fairness—it is about ownership. Where you are right now may not be your fault, but it is your responsibility to rise above it.

Second, take action. Nobody is coming to knock on your door and offer you your dreams. You have to get up and build them yourself. Start where you are, use what you have, and do what you can. Progress is made through effort, discipline, and the relentless pursuit of your goals. Complaining gets you nowhere—consistent action gets you results.

Third, develop resilience. Life will test you. You will face rejection, failure, and setbacks. But winners are not the people who never fail. Instead, they are the people who refuse to stay down. When things go wrong, adjust. When obstacles arise, adapt. But never, ever quit. The moment you realize you are your own rescuer, you become unstoppable.

Fourth, cultivate a mindset of self-reliance. Learn the skills you need. Build the habits that set you up for success. Surround yourself with people who challenge and inspire you. Your success is in your hands—invest in yourself, because nobody else is going to do it for you.

And finally, embrace the power of accountability. Hold yourself to a higher standard. Do not wait for permission, motivation, or perfect conditions. The best time to start was yesterday. The second-best time is now. You are capable. You are strong. But you must decide to take full control of your future.

Will you keep waiting, or will you rise? Will you keep making excuses, or will you take action? Because the truth is, nobody is coming to rescue you—but that is a good thing. Because you do not need rescuing. You have everything within you to build the life you want. It is time to step up, take ownership, and make it happen!

Taking Action

Think | Write | Grow

Based on what you learned in this chapter:

What's something you will stop doing or a habit you will break?

_____

_____

What's something you will start doing or a habit you will create?

_____

_____

What's the potential positive impact of improving in this area?

_____

_____

Chapter Sixteen

Letting Go Is Refusing to Drink Poison

Rival 3: The Past

There is an old saying that holding onto anger and resentment is like drinking poison and expecting the other person to suffer. It is a powerful metaphor because it reveals a truth that many of us fail to recognize—unforgiveness does not harm the person who wronged us—it harms us.

Pain, betrayal, and disappointment are a part of life. We have all been hurt. We have all been let down. And sometimes, the wounds run deep. But when we hold on to resentment, when we replay the pain over and over in our minds, when we refuse to let go, we are the ones who suffer the most. It is like carrying a heavy weight everywhere we go—our energy is drained, our joy is diminished, and our peace is stolen.

The truth is, forgiveness is not about the other person. It is about us. It is about setting ourselves free. It is about choosing peace over pain, healing over bitterness, and freedom over the prison of resentment.

So, why do so many of us struggle to forgive? Because we believe that holding onto anger gives us control. We think that by staying bitter we are somehow protecting ourselves from future hurt. But, in reality, we are doing the opposite. We are keeping ourselves chained to the very thing that hurt us. We are giving the past power over our present. We are drinking poison, expecting someone else to feel its effects.

So, how do we let go? How do we free ourselves from the burden of unforgiveness?

First, we must make a decision. Forgiveness is not about feelings—it is a choice. You may never feel like forgiving. But when you make the decision to release the pain, to stop reliving the past, to let go of the need for revenge, you take the first step toward freedom.

Second, we must understand that forgiveness is not about excusing or justifying what happened. It does not mean that what the other person did was right. It does not mean that they deserve a second chance. Forgiveness is simply saying, "I will no longer allow this pain to control me."

Third, we must shift our focus. When we dwell on the past, we keep ourselves stuck. But when we focus on the present and the future, we open ourselves up to new possibilities. Choose to invest your energy in things that bring you joy, growth, and peace instead of revisiting pain that cannot be undone.

Fourth, we must practice self-compassion. Sometimes, the hardest person to forgive is ourselves. We carry guilt, regret, and shame from past mistakes. But just as we extend grace to others, we must extend it to ourselves. You are not your past. You are not your mistakes. Forgive yourself, learn, and move forward.

And finally, we must recognize that forgiveness is power. It is not weakness. It does not mean surrender. It is an act of strength. It is reclaiming your happiness, your peace, and your life.

What pain are you holding on to? What grudge is weighing you down? What past hurt is stealing your joy? You have a choice. You can continue drinking the poison of bitterness, or you can choose to let go and set yourself free.

Forgiveness is not about them—it is about you. Let go, and watch as your heart becomes lighter, your mind becomes clearer, and your life becomes filled with peace.

Taking Action

Think | Write | Grow

Based on what you learned in this chapter:

What's something you will stop doing or a habit you will break?

_____

_____

What's something you will start doing or a habit you will create?

_____

_____

What's the potential positive impact of improving in this area?

_____

_____

Chapter Seventeen

Storage Units are Short-Term Solutions

Rival 3: The Past

I magine you have a storage unit filled with boxes. Over the years, whenever you encountered pain, disappointment, or betrayal, you didn't deal with it—you just packed it away. Every grudge, every heart-break, every regret—carefully stored, out of sight but never truly gone. At first, this seems like a solution. It keeps the clutter of emotions from overwhelming you in the moment. But as time passes, that storage unit becomes full. It becomes costly. It weighs you down, even though you're no longer carrying the boxes yourself.

Holding onto emotional baggage is just like putting things in storage—it may feel like a short-term fix, but eventually, it becomes a burden you can't ignore. The more you store, the more space it takes up in your mind, your heart, and your life. And just like an overfilled storage unit, one day you will have to open the doors and face everything you've been avoiding.

We all go through experiences that leave scars. We face rejection, failure, loss, and betrayal. And rather than process those emotions, many of us push them aside. "I'll deal with this later," we tell ourselves. But later never comes. Instead, we carry the weight of the past into our present. It affects our relationships, our confidence, and our happiness. And the longer we hold on to it, the heavier it becomes.

So, how do we break free? How do we stop storing emotional baggage and start truly letting go?

First, we must acknowledge what we've been holding onto. Just like cleaning out a cluttered storage unit, we have to open the boxes and take an honest look inside. What unresolved pain are you still carrying? What past hurts have you tucked away? What emotions have you ignored instead of faced? Awareness is the first step to freedom.

Second, we must process and release. Storing emotions doesn't make them disappear—it only postpones the inevitable. If we want to move forward, we must process our pain. That might mean talking to someone we trust, journaling, meditating, or even seeking professional help. Emotions don't heal in storage—they heal when we bring them into the light and deal with them head-on.

Third, we must forgive—not for the sake of others, but for ourselves. Some of the heaviest baggage we carry is resentment and regret. We hold on to past wrongs, replaying them in our minds as if doing so will change the past. But unforgiveness is like paying rent on a storage unit full of things that no longer serve us. The only way to free ourselves is to let go. Forgiveness is not saying what happened was okay—it is saying that you will no longer allow it to take up space in your life.

Fourth, we must make space for new growth. When we finally clean out emotional baggage, we make room for joy, peace, and new possibilities. Think about it—if your storage unit is full of old, useless junk, how can you ever bring in anything new? The same applies to your heart and mind. Let go of what no longer serves you so that you can make space for what truly matters.

And finally, we must commit to ongoing emotional housekeeping. Life will always bring new challenges, new pains, and new experiences. But instead of packing them away, we must learn to deal with emotions as they come. Process them, learn from them, and release them. That way, we never again find ourselves buried under the weight of unhealed wounds. Let go and set yourself free!

Taking Action

Think | Write | Grow

Based on what you learned in this chapter:

What's something you will stop doing or a habit you will break?

_____

_____

What's something you will start doing or a habit you will create?

_____

_____

What's the potential positive impact of improving in this area?

_____

_____

Chapter Eighteen

Both the Young and the Old Succeed

Rival 3: The Past

There is a truth that transcends generations and defies expectations, limitations, and the ticking hands of time. It is this: Success has no age limit. We live in a world that often tells the young, *"You're too inexperienced,"* and the old, *"You're past your prime."* But history—and life itself—tells a different story. Success does not belong to the young or the old. Instead, it belongs to those who dare to chase it and are willing to do the work.

If you are young, you have something extraordinary, such as energy, fresh ideas, and the courage to dream big. The world may doubt your abilities, but let me remind you—some of the greatest successes in history began early. Steve Jobs co-founded Apple at 21. Mark Zuckerberg launched Facebook at 19. Malala Yousafzai became a Nobel laureate at 17.

Their youth was not a limitation—it was fuel for their ambition. But here's the truth: Success at a young age isn't about luck—it's about effort. It's about showing up, learning, failing, and trying again. It's about surrounding yourself with mentors, absorbing wisdom, and having the resilience to rise above challenges. So, if you're young and full of ambition, don't wait for permission to be great. Start now. Fail fast. Learn faster. And never let anyone tell you that you are too young to make an impact.

As for those who have seen more years—those who have walked through decades of experience—you may wonder, *"Is it too late for me?"* And to that, I say absolutely not—when you combine age and experience, you harness the power of wisdom. Colonel Sanders was 65 when he founded

KFC. Vera Wang entered the fashion industry at 40. Nelson Mandela became South Africa's president at 76—and the list goes on. Age is not a barrier—it's an advantage. With years come wisdom, patience, and a deep understanding. If you are older, you bring something that youth cannot—experience. You have seen failures and learned from them. You have developed the type of authentic perseverance that only time can teach.

Your age is your power. Your experiences have shaped you. If you are 50, 60, 70, or beyond, you still have time to build, to inspire, and to achieve great things. Success is not about when you start—it's about the decision to start. Remember that whether young or old, what truly matters is grit and the type of drive that cannot be tamed because it is fueled by passion. Grit is the ability to push through failures. Passion fuels the fire to keep going, and purpose gives meaning to the work you choose to do. If you have the courage to start, the discipline to continue, and the resilience to rise after every fall—success can be yours.

So, to the young—dream big, but work hard. Learn from those who have come before you. Your potential is limitless. And to the seasoned—your best years are not behind you—they are within you. Share your wisdom, pursue your passions, and prove that age is just a number. Because, in the end, success is not about age. It is about action. Make today your time to shine.

Taking Action

Think | Write | Grow

Based on what you learned in this chapter:

What's something you will stop doing or a habit you will break?

_____

_____

What's something you will start doing or a habit you will create?

_____

_____

What's the potential positive impact of improving in this area?

_____

_____

Chapter Nineteen

Comparing Me to Myself Is Reasonable

Rival 3: The Past

Today, we live in a world where it's easier than ever to compare ourselves to others. We scroll through social media and see someone with a bigger house, a better job, a more exciting life. We hear about people our age—maybe younger—achieving success, and we wonder, "Why not me?" The truth is, comparison steals joy, weakens confidence, and holds us back from reaching our true potential. It distracts you from your own path and blinds you to your own progress. When you focus on others, you lose focus of your greatest competitor, which is the person you were yesterday.

Think about it this way—when you take the bait of comparing yourself to others, you're comparing your behind-the-scenes to their highlight reel. You don't see their struggles, their sleepless nights, or their failures. You only see their victories. And the truth is, there will always be someone ahead of you. Someone faster, richer, more talented. But does that mean you're failing? Absolutely not. It just means you're on a different path. Each of us has our own timeline. Your journey is yours alone, and it's not meant to look like anyone else's. Success isn't about being better than someone else—it's about being better than your former self—the person you used to be.

Imagine if every day, you wake up and ask yourself, "How can I be just 1% better than yesterday?" Can I be a little kinder? Can I work a little harder? Can I push myself just a little more? When you focus on your own growth, amazing things happen. You start seeing progress—not based on someone else's life, but based on your own improvement. You become unstoppable when you give your attention to your own forward progress, no matter how small.

Make each day about growth and progress, not perfection. Maybe yesterday, you stumbled or remained in neutral. Maybe last week you failed. That's okay! Because success isn't about avoiding failure—it's about learning from it. Get into the habit of viewing every setback as a lesson and an opportunity, and every day as a fresh start, and watch what happens. Instead of asking, "Am I as successful as they are?" Ask yourself, "Am I learning, growing, and improving?" Because that's the type of introspection that leads to success and well-being.

So, how do we stop comparing ourselves to others? Here are three things to remember:

Focus On Your Own Lane: Imagine running a race. If you keep looking at the person next to you, you'll slow down. Stay in your lane. Keep moving forward. Your journey is yours, and yours alone.

Measure Progress, Not Perfection: Instead of asking, "Am I as good as them?" Ask, "Am I better than I was yesterday?" Small improvements add up to massive success.

Celebrate Others Without Doubting Yourself: Just because someone else is winning doesn't mean you're losing. Life is not a competition—it's a journey. Their success doesn't take away from yours.

At the end of the day, you don't need to be better than anyone else. You just need to be the best version of you, which is accomplished one step at a time by doing a little better than you did yesterday. So, eliminate the trap of comparison once and for all. Let go of self-doubt and focus your attention on growth, learning, and becoming the best version of yourself. When you stop looking at others and start focusing on your own path, you will have harnessed one of the master keys to lasting success.

Taking Action

Think | Write | Grow

Based on what you learned in this chapter:

What's something you will stop doing or a habit you will break?

_____

_____

What's something you will start doing or a habit you will create?

_____

_____

What's the potential positive impact of improving in this area?

_____

_____

Chapter Twenty

Guilt and Shame Are Good in Moderation

Rival 3: The Past

G uilt and shame are often spoken of interchangeably, but they are profoundly different in their impact on our minds, our actions, and our sense of self-worth. The difference between these two words is subtle but powerful. Guilt says, "I did something bad." Shame says, "I am bad." Guilt focuses on behavior, while shame attacks identity. And that difference can determine whether we grow from our mistakes or allow them to define us.

Guilt, in its healthiest form, is a signal. It is a nudge from our conscience, telling us we have acted in a way that goes against our values or the expectations we hold for ourselves. It is uncomfortable—but it is also constructive. It can push us to apologize, to make amends, to reflect on our choices, and to improve. Think about the last time you felt guilty. Maybe you said something in anger that you didn't mean. Maybe you failed to keep a promise to someone who trusted you. Maybe you ignored an opportunity to help someone when you could have. That feeling of guilt, if managed correctly, isn't there to break you down—it's there to make you better. It tells you that you care and that you are still connected to your values, which is a good thing.

Now, let's contrast that with shame. Shame isn't about a mistake you made—it's about believing that you, as a person, are unworthy, inadequate, or fundamentally flawed. Shame is the voice that says, "I'm not good enough." It's the thought that tells you that no matter what you do, you will never be deserving of love, respect, or forgiveness. Shame is destructive because it doesn't inspire change—it paralyzes us. When we feel shame, we don't see a path forward. We don't see an opportunity to fix what went wrong because we don't believe we are capable of change. And worst of all, shame isolates us. It makes us hide from others, from ourselves, and from the very lessons that could help us grow.

So, how do we make sure that guilt helps us grow while shame doesn't hold us back?

First, we must recognize that making mistakes does not make us bad people. Everyone has failed, has hurt someone, and fallen short of their best self at some point. That doesn't mean we are unworthy—it means we are human. The difference between those who move forward and those who stay stuck is how they respond to their mistakes.

Second, we must learn to separate what we do from who we are. If you make a mistake, own it, but don't let it define you. If you hurt someone, apologize, but don't believe you are irredeemable. If you fail at something important to you, try again.

Finally, we must remind ourselves that growth is the only real measure of success. A person who never experiences guilt has either never made a mistake—or has stopped listening to their conscience. But a person who lets shame control them has lost faith in their own self-worth.

So, the next time you feel guilt, embrace it as a teacher. Ask yourself, "What can I learn from this?" The next time you feel shame creeping in, challenge it. Remind yourself that no mistake, no failure, no moment of weakness can take away your inherent value. Guilt can be a guide. Shame is a trap. The choice is ours. Will we let our past mistakes shape our future growth, or will we let them define our worth?

Taking Action

Think | Write | Grow

Based on what you learned in this chapter:

What's something you will stop doing or a habit you will break?

_____

_____

What's something you will start doing or a habit you will create?

_____

_____

What's the potential positive impact of improving in this area?

_____

_____

Chapter Twenty-One

Taking Ownership Is Empowerment

Rival 3: The Past

Let's be honest. No one likes to be wrong. No one enjoys making mistakes. Our natural instinct is to protect ourselves, to defend our actions, or even to shift the blame. Sometimes, we blame circumstances. Sometimes, we blame others. And sometimes, we go into denial, convincing ourselves that the mistake never happened at all. But here's the hard truth: blaming others or denying our mistakes keeps us weak. Taking ownership makes us strong.

When we take ownership of our mistakes, we are no longer victims of our circumstances. We are in control. Think about it: if everything is someone else's fault, then we have no power to change our situation. We stay stuck, waiting for other people or outside forces to fix things for us. But when we say, "This is on me. I made this mistake, and I will fix it," we regain control of our lives. Taking ownership is not about beating ourselves up. It's not about feeling guilty forever or dwelling on what went wrong. It's about using our mistakes as stepping stones to grow, improve, and become better.

Every great leader, every successful person, every inspiring individual you know has made mistakes. The difference is how they handled them. Think about some of the greatest minds in history—Thomas Edison, who failed a thousand times before inventing the light bulb. Michael Jordan, who was cut from the high school basketball team. Steve Jobs, who was removed from the very company he founded. None of them let their failures define them. They owned their mistakes, learned from them, and came back stronger.

Now, imagine if Edison had blamed his tools. Imagine if Jordan had blamed his height. Imagine if Steve Jobs had stayed bitter and never returned to Apple. The world would be missing some of its greatest innovations. Mistakes are not the end of the road. They are simply lessons in disguise. But we only learn the lesson when we take responsibility.

There is something liberating about taking ownership. The moment you say, "This was my mistake, and I take full responsibility," you free yourself from the burden of excuses. You stop wasting energy on justifying, denying, or pointing fingers. Instead, you direct that energy toward growth, toward finding solutions, and toward becoming the best version of yourself.

Let's take a common example—relationships. Whether it's in the workplace, at home, or with friends, conflicts happen. If we always blame the other person, the problem never gets solved. But when we have the courage to say, "I could have handled that better. I was wrong," we build trust. We strengthen our relationships. People respect those who can admit their faults because it shows integrity and character.

So, how do we practice ownership in our daily lives?

First, we acknowledge the mistake. Stop making excuses. Stop justifying. Simply say, "I was wrong." Second, we learn from it. Every mistake is a lesson. Ask yourself, "What can I do differently next time?" Third, we do our best to make it right. If your mistake hurt someone, apologize. If it caused a problem, find a way to fix it. Actions speak louder than words. Last, move forward. Don't dwell on the past. Simply learn, improve, and keep going.

The people who achieve the most in life are not the ones who never fail. They are the ones who own their failures and use them to fuel their growth. They don't waste time blaming others or hiding from the truth. They step up. They take responsibility. And because of that, they rise above the challenges that hold others back. Remember this: ownership is power. Responsibility is freedom. And every mistake is a chance to become stronger than before.

Taking Action

Think | Write | Grow

Based on what you learned in this chapter:

What's something you will stop doing or a habit you will break?

_____

_____

What's something you will start doing or a habit you will create?

_____

_____

What's the potential positive impact of improving in this area?

_____

_____

RIVAL 4

I D L E N E S S

"Take Action Now"

Chapter Twenty-Two

Motivation Is the Result of Action

Rival 4: Idleness

How many times have you waited to "feel" motivated before taking action? Maybe you've wanted to start working out, but you told yourself, *"I'll do it when I feel more motivated."* Maybe you've wanted to start a project, a business, or a new habit, but you've been waiting for that burst of inspiration, that perfect moment when motivation just kicks in. But here's the truth: Motivation doesn't create action. Action creates motivation. If we only acted when we felt like it, we'd get nowhere. The people who succeed, who grow, who push past their limits—they don't wait to feel motivated. They take action first.

Too many people believe motivation is something that just happens to us, like a lightning bolt from the sky. They think successful people are constantly inspired, always energized, and always ready to go. That's not true. Even the most successful people in the world have days when they don't feel like showing up. What separates them from the rest? They show up anyway.

Think about an athlete training for a competition. Do you think they feel excited every single morning when the alarm goes off before sunrise? No, but they lace up their shoes and hit the gym anyway. Think about an inspiring author working on their first book. Do you think they feel inspired to write every day? No, but they sit down and write anyway. Successful people have learned that motivation is not a feeling or emotion—it's something that can only be built through action.

Here's the secret: The hardest part is starting. Have you ever noticed that once you begin something—whether it's a workout, a difficult task, or a project—you start feeling more engaged? That's because action creates momentum, and momentum fuels motivation. When you take the first step, even when you don't feel like it, something incredible happens: Your mind shifts from resistance to focus, your body starts to engage, and you begin to see progress, which fuels more action.

The first five minutes of anything is the hardest. But once you push through that resistance, you prove to yourself that you are capable. If action creates motivation, then what gets us to take action in the first place? Discipline! Discipline is doing what needs to be done, even when you don't feel like it. It's showing up for yourself, not because of a mood or a feeling, but because of a commitment you made to yourself. Motivation is temporary—it comes and goes. Discipline is consistent—it stays with you. If you only work hard when you feel like it, you'll be inconsistent. But if you develop the discipline to take action, no matter how you feel, you'll always move forward.

To build self-motivation through action, start small. Don't wait for the perfect moment. Start with five minutes. Five minutes of exercise. Five minutes of writing. Five minutes of effort. Once you start, you'll often keep going. Focus on the process, not the feeling. Instead of asking, *"Do I feel like doing this?"* ask, *"What needs to be done?"*

Remove the option to quit. Don't negotiate with yourself. Don't allow excuses. Make action a non-negotiable part of your day. Celebrate Progress. Every small step matters. Recognize that motivation grows when you see results—no matter how small. Lastly, trust yourself. Remind yourself that feelings are temporary, but actions create real change. Self-motivation isn't about waiting for inspiration. It's about showing up for yourself, even on the hard days. It's about taking action first and letting motivation catch up.

What have you been waiting to feel motivated to do? What's that one thing you've been putting off, waiting for the perfect moment? Stop waiting. Take action today, because action is the key to momentum, and momentum is the key to success!

Taking Action

Think | Write | Grow

Based on what you learned in this chapter:

What's something you will stop doing or a habit you will break?

_____

_____

What's something you will start doing or a habit you will create?

_____

_____

What's the potential positive impact of improving in this area?

_____

_____

Chapter Twenty-Three

Habits Are the Manifestation of Beliefs

Rival 4: Idleness

I f I were to ask you, "What *do you believe about yourself?*" How would you answer? Maybe you'd say, *I believe I am hardworking. I believe I am disciplined. I believe I am capable.* But here's the question: Do your daily habits reflect those beliefs? Because the truth is, our habits are the clearest evidence of what we truly believe—not what we say we believe, not what we hope to believe, but what we actually believe deep down.

If someone believes they are a healthy person, what do they do? They exercise, they eat well, and they prioritize rest. If someone believes they are a leader, what do they do? They take initiative, they hold themselves accountable, and they strive to grow. If someone believes they are a failure, what do they do? They procrastinate, they avoid challenges, and they don't push themselves. See, we don't just act according to our habits—our habits reveal who we think we are.

James Clear, the author of *Atomic Habits*, says, *"Every action is a vote for the type of person you want to become."* That means every time you wake up early to work on your goals, you're casting a vote that says, *I am disciplined.* Every time you push yourself to do that extra rep at the gym, you're casting a vote that says, *I am strong.* Every time you show up when it would have been easier to quit, you're reinforcing the belief that *I am unstoppable.*

The problem is, many of us have habits that contradict what we say we believe. You might say, *I want to be successful,* but if your daily habits include hitting the snooze button, procrastinating, and making excuses, your actions say otherwise. You might say, *I want to be confident,* but if your habits include negative self-talk, avoiding risks, and staying in your comfort zone, what do you really believe? It's not about shame. It's about awareness. Because once you see the disconnect between your beliefs and your habits, you have the power to change it.

Here are some ways to create productive habits:

First, don't just set goals. Ask yourself, *Who is the person I want to become?* Do you want to be a disciplined person? A confident leader? A resilient warrior? Define it.

Second, audit your daily habits. Look at your routine. Are your daily actions supporting the identity you want to build? If you want to be strong, are you training? If you want to be wise, are you reading? If you want to be successful, are you putting in the work?

Third, big transformations don't happen overnight. They happen through small, consistent actions. If you want to be a writer, start writing one page a day. If you want to be fit, commit to a 10-minute workout.

Fourth, stop saying, *I want to be disciplined.* Start saying, *I am disciplined.* Every action that aligns with this belief makes it stronger. The more you act like the person you want to become, the more you start believing it.

At the end of the day, success, confidence, discipline—they don't come from one big moment. They come from the small, daily choices we make over and over again. Your habits are not just routines. They are the physical proof of what you truly believe about yourself. So I leave you with this challenge: What do your habits say about you? And, more importantly, are they aligned with the person you truly want to be? Because if they're not, today is the day to change that.

Taking Action

Think | Write | Grow

Based on what you learned in this chapter:

What's something you will stop doing or a habit you will break?

_____

_____

What's something you will start doing or a habit you will create?

_____

_____

What's the potential positive impact of improving in this area?

_____

_____

Chapter Twenty-Four

What Gets Measured Gets Improved

Rival 4: Idleness

S etting goals is essential for success, but not all goals are created equal. Many people set broad aspirations like "get in shape" or "be successful" without defining clear steps to get there. The key to achieving meaningful progress lies in setting measurable goals—ones that can be tracked with daily and weekly milestones.

When you set goals that can be measured, you create a roadmap for success. Instead of just hoping for a better future, you take intentional, actionable steps toward it. This method keeps you focused, motivated, and adaptable. Measurable goals matter. Breaking them down into daily and weekly milestones can significantly enhance your productivity and long-term success. Put simply, a goal without a plan is just a wish. If you don't measure progress, it's easy to lose momentum or feel overwhelmed.

Here are four things you can do to increase your chances of crossing the finish line of the goals that you start:

Track Progress: Seeing how far you've come gives you motivation to keep going.

Stay Accountable: When you track results, you hold yourself (or those who have asked you) accountable.

Adjust and Improve: If something isn't working, you can make changes before it's too late.

Stay Focused: Clear milestones help eliminate distractions and keep you on track.

Setting a big goal is inspiring, but it can also feel daunting. That's why breaking it down into smaller, achievable milestones is so important. Daily milestones should comprise small, actionable steps that push you forward every day. They provide structure, helping you form productive habits. Weekly milestones help you measure progress over a slightly longer timeframe, ensuring you're moving in the right direction. By tracking both, you create a steady rhythm of achievement and self-motivation, reducing the chances of procrastination or burnout.

To create goals that can be measured and tracked, consider following the SMART framework:

Specific: Clearly define what you want to achieve.

Measurable: Identify how you will track progress.

Achievable: Make sure the goal is realistic.

Relevant: Align it with your bigger vision.

Time-Bound: Set deadlines to keep yourself accountable.

For example, instead of saying, "I want to get in shape," set a SMART goal like: "I will work out for 30 minutes, five times a week, for the next three months." Now you have a clear, measurable target that can be tracked with daily and weekly milestones.

By following this structured approach, you make steady progress without feeling overwhelmed. To stay on top of your progress, use tools like journals and planners to write daily and weekly targets. Use apps and software to track your progress. Share your progress with a mentor or peer.

In conclusion, setting measurable goals and tracking them with daily and weekly milestones is a game-changer. It transforms vague ambitions into clear, achievable actions, ensuring that you stay focused, accountable, and motivated. By breaking big dreams into smaller, trackable steps, you build momentum and set yourself up for long-term success. Whether in business, health, or personal growth, this strategy will help you turn aspirations into reality—one milestone at a time. What's one goal you can start tracking today?

Taking Action

Think | Write | Grow

Based on what you learned in this chapter:

What's something you will stop doing or a habit you will break?

_____

_____

What's something you will start doing or a habit you will create?

_____

_____

What's the potential positive impact of improving in this area?

_____

_____

Chapter Twenty-Five

Visualization Precedes Actualization

Rival 4: Idleness

I want to share with you a powerful tool that has the potential to transform your aspirations into achievements, which is visualization. This practice, often referred to as mental imagery or creative visualization, involves creating vivid mental pictures of your desired outcomes. It's more than mere daydreaming—it's a deliberate technique that can bridge the gap between your current reality and your dreams.

Research has shown that visualization activates the same neural pathways in the brain as actual physical performance. This means that when we vividly imagine ourselves achieving a goal, our brain processes it similarly to real-life execution. This mental rehearsal strengthens neural connections, enhancing our skills and boosting confidence.

Visualization isn't confined to theoretical studies—it's a practical tool employed by high achievers across various fields. For instance, athletes often use visualization to enhance performance by mentally rehearsing their routines, which can lead to improved outcomes.

There are three significant benefits of visualization, with the first being enhanced motivation, because it can stimulate enthusiasm and perseverance toward goals. Second, mental rehearsal can lead to better performance in various tasks. Third, it can reduce stress and anxiety levels, contributing to overall well-being.

Practical Steps to Effective Visualization

1. Define Clear Goals: Begin by setting specific, measurable, achievable, relevant, and time-bound (SMART) goals. A clear

target provides direction for your visualization.

2. Engage All Senses: When visualizing, incorporate all five senses. Imagine not just the sights but also the sounds, smells, tastes, and tactile sensations associated with your success. This multisensory approach makes the visualization more vivid and impactful.

3. Practice Regularly: Dedicate time daily to your visualization practice. Consistency reinforces neural pathways, making the envisioned outcome more familiar and attainable.

4. Combine with Action: Visualization is a powerful tool, but it must be paired with concrete actions. Use the motivation and clarity gained from visualization to drive your daily efforts toward your goals.

Visualization also serves as a powerful tool to overcome obstacles. By mentally rehearsing how to navigate potential challenges, we prepare ourselves to handle them with resilience and poise. This proactive approach reduces anxiety and builds confidence, as our minds become familiar with confronting and overcoming difficulties.

The benefits of visualization extend beyond individual achievements. As we realize our goals, we inspire those around us, creating a ripple effect of motivation and positivity. Our success stories become testimonies to the power of the mind, encouraging others to harness their imagination for personal and collective growth.

Visualization is a bridge between our current reality and our desired future. By vividly imagining our goals, engaging our senses, and coupling our visions with deliberate actions, we set the stage for actualization. Remember, every achievement begins as a thought. Nurture those thoughts with clarity and purpose, and watch as they transform into tangible realities.

Taking Action

Think | Write | Grow

Based on what you learned in this chapter:

What's something you will stop doing or a habit you will break?

_____

_____

What's something you will start doing or a habit you will create?

_____

_____

What's the potential positive impact of improving in this area?

_____

_____

Chapter Twenty-Six

Talkers Accept Payment in Advance

Rival 4: Idleness

I want to share a counterintuitive insight that could transform the way you approach your aspirations. While setting goals is a fundamental step toward achieving success, publicly announcing these goals can paradoxically diminish your chances of realizing them. Let's delve into why keeping your ambitions private might be the key to unlocking your full potential.

The Dopamine Deception: Premature Satisfaction

When you share your goals with others, the acknowledgment and praise you receive can create a false sense of accomplishment. This phenomenon is rooted in our brain's reward system. Discussing your intentions triggers a release of dopamine, the "feel-good" neurotransmitter, leading you to feel rewarded without having made tangible progress. As a result, your motivation to pursue the actual work required diminishes. This concept is supported by research highlighted in *Psychology Today*, which explains that our brain can be tricked into feeling that the goal has been achieved upon sharing it, reducing the energy invested in further implementation. This dopamine deception creates a sense of premature satisfaction and has the potential of derailing goals before critical momentum is achieved.

Announcing your goals can create an illusion of progress. You might feel that by merely articulating your objectives, you're moving closer to them. However, this verbal affirmation can replace the satisfaction that should come from actual achievements, leading to complacency. As noted in *Inc.com*, telling others about your goals can give you a premature sense of completeness, thereby reducing your drive to work toward them.

Psychologists have identified the "over justification effect," where external reinforcement, such as social acknowledgment, can undermine intrinsic motivation. When your internal drive is overshadowed by external validation, your commitment to the goal weakens. This shift from internal to external motivation can be detrimental to sustained effort and perseverance.

Keeping your goals private can enhance your commitment to them. When you resist the urge to share, you maintain the internal pressure to achieve, relying solely on your intrinsic motivation. This self-reliance fosters resilience and a stronger personal connection to your objectives.

To be successful, you must choose actions over words. Clearly define what you aim to achieve and outline actionable steps. Document your journey privately, allowing for self-reflection and continuous improvement. Instead of broadly announcing your goals, confide in a trusted individual who can provide support and honest feedback. Celebrate milestones internally, acknowledge your progress personally, and reinforce your intrinsic motivation without external validation.

In a world that often encourages sharing every detail of our lives, choosing to keep your goals private can be a powerful strategy for success. By doing so, you preserve your intrinsic motivation, avoid the pitfalls of premature satisfaction, and maintain a clear focus on the actions necessary to achieve your dreams. Remember, it's the quiet, consistent efforts that lead to meaningful accomplishments.

Taking Action

Think | Write | Grow

Based on what you learned in this chapter:

What's something you will stop doing or a habit you will break?

_____

_____

What's something you will start doing or a habit you will create?

_____

_____

What's the potential positive impact of improving in this area?

_____

_____

Chapter Twenty-Seven

Success Requires Deliberate Sacrifice

Rival 4: Idleness

O ne of the most fundamental truths about success is that it requires consistent and deliberate sacrifice. This concept may seem daunting, but understanding and embracing it can be the key to unlocking your full potential. At its core, sacrifice involves giving up something valuable or necessary to achieve a larger purpose. Pursuing success often means sacrificing time, money, comfort, relationships, and even personal desires because you know there is something greater out there. It may seem daunting and overwhelming at first, but it's essential to achieving any form of success.

Sacrifice forces you to prioritize. When you sacrifice, you understand that not everything can be attained or done simultaneously. You must make hard choices and prioritize what is truly important to achieve your goals. This helps in avoiding distractions and staying focused on what really matters. Sacrifice requires self-discipline and resilience. It takes an iron will to give up short-term gratification for long-term gain. By sacrificing, you develop the mental strength necessary to overcome challenges and persevere in the face of all obstacles.

Sacrifice is a powerful motivator. When you pay for something, you tend to value that thing much more. When you pay the price, you tend to value the trade in terms of your cost. When you sacrifice, it's like making payments for something in the future. Instant gratification is the true epidemic of our time. We want everything now, instantly. But the things that truly matter and lead to long-term success require time and sacrifice. Delaying gratification is crucial for success because instant gratification fosters weakness and powerlessness. The more you sacrifice, the more powerful and capable you become.

Sacrifice comes in various forms, and what one person may consider a sacrifice may not be the same for someone else. It could require giving up personal time to work on a project, cutting down on expenses to save money for an investment, or even sacrificing sleep to complete a task. It is also important to note that sacrifice does not mean giving up something forever. It could mean postponing gratification for a certain period to achieve tremendous success.

Many successful people attribute their success to the sacrifices they were willing to make. For example, Jeff Bezos, the founder of Amazon, was willing to invest all his savings and leave his stable job to start a company that would eventually become one of the biggest e-commerce platforms. There are countless stories of those who were determined and willing to make sacrifices to achieve their goals, and they serve as an inspiration for others who are on the path to success.

While sacrifices may be difficult in the short term, they often lead to long-term benefits. Sacrificing now for a better future can result in financial stability, personal growth, and overall happiness. Moreover, the sacrifices we make today can also positively affect future generations. By setting an example of hard work and determination, we inspire others to strive for success and make sacrifices.

Achieving success is a journey paved with consistent and deliberate sacrifices. By embracing this reality, you position yourself to overcome challenges and attain your aspirations. Remember, the sacrifices you make today are the investments in your successful tomorrow.

Taking Action

Think | Write | Grow

Based on what you learned in this chapter:

What's something you will stop doing or a habit you will break?

_____

_____

What's something you will start doing or a habit you will create?

_____

_____

What's the potential positive impact of improving in this area?

_____

_____

Chapter Twenty-Eight

When It's Resolute, It Begins Before Sunrise

Rival 4: Idleness

I cannot overemphasize a simple yet profound truth: The perfect time to start working on your dreams and goals is now. Too often, we find ourselves waiting for the "right" moment—a moment when circumstances align perfectly, when we feel absolutely ready, or when external conditions seem ideal. However, this notion of a perfect time is an illusion that can hinder our progress and keep us stagnant.

Waiting for the perfect moment often leads to perpetual postponement. Life is inherently unpredictable, and waiting for all variables to align flawlessly is an exercise in futility. As highlighted in an article from *Inc.com*, delaying the pursuit of your dreams can make the journey harder, not easier. The longer we wait, the more we risk entrenching ourselves in comfort zones, making it increasingly challenging to take that first crucial step.

Starting today, regardless of how small the step, sets a powerful precedent. It transforms abstract aspirations into tangible actions. Each action, no matter how minor, builds momentum. This momentum not only propels us forward but also fosters a sense of accomplishment, reinforcing our commitment to our goals.

One of the primary reasons we delay action is the fear of failure. We worry about the uncertainties and potential setbacks. However, it's essential to recognize that failure is not the opposite of success but a part of it. Each misstep offers valuable lessons, refining our strategies and strengthening our resolve. By embracing the possibility of failure, we liberate ourselves from the paralysis of over-analysis and open the door to growth and resilience.

Procrastination is a subtle thief of time and potential. It lulls us into a false sense of security, making us believe that there's always tomorrow. However, as highlighted by *The Financial Diet*, perpetually waiting for the right moment can be a dangerous path, leading to missed opportunities and unfulfilled potential. By recognizing the pitfalls of procrastination, we can take proactive steps to counteract it, such as setting clear deadlines and holding ourselves accountable.

Beginning today allows for the gradual development of skills necessary to achieve your goals. With time, these skills compound, leading to mastery and increased confidence. Early challenges teach adaptability and resilience, while facing obstacles equips us with the problem-solving abilities needed for long-term success. Taking initiative and action opens doors to unforeseen opportunities and attracts possibilities that remain hidden during inaction. The journey of pursuing our goals fosters personal development, enriching our lives with experiences and insights that shape our character and worldview.

The journey to realizing our dreams and goals begins with a single step taken right now. By dismissing the myth of the perfect moment and embracing immediate action, we set ourselves on a path of continuous growth and fulfillment. Remember, time will pass regardless, so it's up to us to decide how we use it. So, let's commit to our aspirations now, for the only true obstacle between us and our dreams is the decision to start.

Taking Action

Think | Write | Grow

Based on what you learned in this chapter:

What's something you will stop doing or a habit you will break?

_____

_____

What's something you will start doing or a habit you will create?

_____

_____

What's the potential positive impact of improving in this area?

_____

_____

RIVAL 5

--- ◆ ---

A D V E R S I T Y

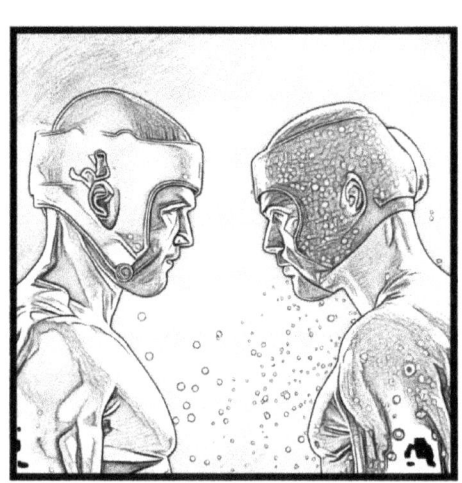

"Claim Your Power"

Chapter Twenty-Nine

Beware of the Path Without Obstacles

Rival 5: Adversity

I t's important that we reflect on a profound truth regarding the journey towards authentic success, which teaches us that paths without obstacles seldom lead to significant destinations. This concept, encapsulated by the quote, "If you find a path with no obstacles, it probably doesn't lead anywhere," attributed to Frank A. Clark, serves as a powerful reminder of the role challenges play in our journey toward meaningful achievements.

Obstacles are inherent to any worthwhile endeavor. They are not mere hindrances but essential components of the growth process. Each challenge we encounter compels us to adapt, innovate, and evolve. As highlighted in an article from Harper Therapy, obstacles provide valuable life lessons and opportunities to cultivate qualities like determination, patience, adaptability, and empathy.

Facing and overcoming obstacles is integral to personal development. Each challenge tests our resolve, refines our skills, and builds resilience. The process of navigating difficulties fosters a deeper understanding of our capabilities and limitations, leading to enhanced self-awareness and confidence. When it comes to consistently overcoming obstacles and achieving success, determination is a crucial trait that drives us to persist through challenges, ultimately leading to personal and professional growth.

Challenges often serve as catalysts for creativity and innovation. When the familiar path is blocked, we are compelled to explore alternative routes, leading to new ideas and solutions. This powerful perspective has been echoed in my personal and professional life countless times, emphasizing that implementing, adapting, and taking action with the right mindset enables us to overcome obstacles and find success.

Resilience is forged in the crucible of adversity. Each obstacle we confront and surmount strengthens our ability to face future challenges with greater fortitude. This cumulative process equips us with the mental and emotional tools necessary to navigate the complexities of life. As highlighted in the lives of of those who have made the tumultuous journey from rags to riches, overcoming obstacles fosters growth and is essential for achieving personal and professional fulfillment because a higher value is placed on success that has been fought for and earned.

It's essential to recognize that the presence of obstacles is not indicative of a misguided path but rather a sign that we are on a journey worthwhile of our undertaking. Embracing challenges with a positive mindset transforms potential roadblocks into stepping stones toward our goals, dreams, and aspirations. Obstacles push us to examine our beliefs, clarify values, and develop creative problem-solving skills—all of which become powerful life skills.

Remember that the paths we choose in life are seldom devoid of challenges. However, it is through these very obstacles that we find opportunities for growth, innovation, ultimate success, and, in some cases, lifelong friends. Embracing the difficulties along our journey not only enriches our experiences but also leads us to destinations of profound significance. Remember, a path without obstacles likely leads nowhere, but a path embraced with challenges leads to a life well-lived.

Taking Action

Think | Write | Grow

Based on what you learned in this chapter:

What's something you will stop doing or a habit you will break?

_____

_____

What's something you will start doing or a habit you will create?

_____

_____

What's the potential positive impact of improving in this area?

_____

_____

Chapter Thirty

Change and Transition Promote Growth

Rival 5: Adversity

C hange, transition, and uncertainty are forces that shape our personal lives, influence our professional journeys, and define the broader societal landscape. Embracing them is not merely a necessity but an opportunity for growth and innovation. As noted by Heraclitus, "The only constant in life is change." From technological advancements to shifts in global dynamics, change is perpetual. This reality compels us to adapt and evolve continually.

While change refers to external events, transition is the internal process we undergo to adapt to new circumstances. William Bridges, a renowned expert on change, emphasized that transition involves three phases, which are letting go of the old, navigating the neutral zone, and embracing the new beginning. Recognizing and understanding these phases can facilitate smoother adjustments during periods of change.

Uncertainty often accompanies change and transition, bringing feelings of ambiguity and unpredictability. However, uncertainty also presents opportunities for innovation and resilience. Embracing uncertainty with an open mind that is free from irrational fear can lead to transformative outcomes by challenging conventional thinking and encouraging diverse perspectives.

In times of transition and uncertainty, maintaining a positive mindset is crucial. Viewing challenges as opportunities for growth fosters resilience. When you adopt a mindset of possibility and abundance, you metaphorically transform setbacks into stepping stones toward success.

Here are four things you can do to navigate change and transition like a pro:

First, cultivate resilience. Developing resilience enables us to recover from setbacks and adapt to new situations.

Second, foster adaptability. Being open to new ideas and flexible in our approaches allows us to navigate changing landscapes effectively.

Third, enhance communication: Transparent and empathetic communication builds trust and ensures alignment during transitions.

Fourth, commit to continuous learning: Embracing a growth mindset and seeking new knowledge equips us to handle unforeseen challenges.

It's also important to point out that effective leadership is paramount during periods of change and uncertainty. Leaders who demonstrate empathy, decisiveness, and vision can inspire confidence and guide their organizations through turbulent times. Assembling a strong leadership team and embracing uncertainty are vital components of navigating transitions successfully.

While uncertainty can be daunting, it also serves as a catalyst for innovation. When outcomes are not predetermined, there is room for creativity and exploration. Embracing uncertainty allows us to break free from traditional constraints and discover novel solutions to complex problems.

In embracing change, transition, and uncertainty, we unlock the potential for personal growth, organizational success, and societal advancement. By fostering resilience, adaptability, effective communication, and a commitment to continuous learning, we can navigate the complexities of our ever-evolving world with confidence and optimism. Let us view these forces not as threats but as opportunities to innovate, transform, and thrive.

Taking Action

Think | Write | Grow

Based on what you learned in this chapter:

What's something you will stop doing or a habit you will break?

_____

_____

What's something you will start doing or a habit you will create?

_____

_____

What's the potential positive impact of improving in this area?

_____

_____

Chapter Thirty-One

Facing Adversity Earns Expert Power

Rival 5: Adversity

E mbracing adversity is not merely about enduring challenges—it's about transforming them into the rungs of a ladder that leads toward personal mastery and influence. When we confront difficulties head-on, we cultivate resilience, deepen our expertise, and earn the respect that empowers us to lead and inspire others.

Adversity is an inherent part of the human experience. It presents itself in various forms—personal losses, professional setbacks, health challenges, or unforeseen obstacles. While our instinct might urge us to avoid these hardships, it's through facing them that we uncover our true potential. Adversity and the struggles that come with it make us stronger, empowering us to achieve our aspirations.

Confronting adversity head-on fosters resilience. Each challenge we face and overcome enhances our ability to navigate future obstacles with greater confidence and composure. This resilience is not just about bouncing back—it's about growing stronger and more adept, enabling us to handle increasingly complex situations. Facing initial failures with resilience, we can experience significant personal growth, reframing our approach to difficult experiences.

Every adversity carries within it the seeds of learning and growth. When we tackle challenges, we acquire new skills, insights, and perspectives that enrich our personal and professional lives. This process of overcoming difficulties not only enhances our competence but also builds what is known as "expert power." Expert power arises from possessing specialized knowledge or skills that others recognize and value, granting us influence and authority in our respective fields.

Leaders who have navigated adversity and emerged with enhanced expertise wield a unique form of influence. Their journeys through hardship serve as powerful narratives that inspire and motivate others. This form of leadership, grounded in personal experience and resilience, fosters trust and credibility. As noted by American Express, building expert power requires ongoing learning, a willingness to share knowledge, and the ability to apply expertise to real-world challenges.

When leaders openly share their experiences of overcoming adversity, they create a culture of transparency and authenticity. This openness encourages team members to view challenges as opportunities for growth rather than insurmountable obstacles. Such an environment not only enhances individual resilience but also strengthens the collective capability of the organization. Expert power can inspire those around you to develop their own advanced skill sets and areas of expertise.

Choosing to embrace adversity is a conscious decision to pursue growth and excellence. It requires a mindset that views challenges not as threats but as catalysts for development. This perspective shift enables us to extract valuable lessons from hardships, fostering continuous improvement and innovation. Experiencing adversity can lead to increased resilience, making us better equipped to handle future challenges.

Learn to view adversity not a detour from the path to success, but as the path itself. By embracing challenges, we cultivate resilience, transform hardships into expertise, and earn the power to influence and lead others effectively. Let us welcome adversity as a valuable teacher, guiding us toward personal mastery and the ability to inspire those around us.

Taking Action

Think | Write | Grow

Based on what you learned in this chapter:

What's something you will stop doing or a habit you will break?

_____

_____

What's something you will start doing or a habit you will create?

_____

_____

What's the potential positive impact of improving in this area?

_____

_____

Chapter Thirty-Two

Harsh Conditions Will Cull the Herd

Rival 5: Adversity

Life, at its core, is not endless comfort. It is a changing season—storms, droughts, winters so cold they test the very marrow of our bones. And it is in those harsh conditions, in the brutal adversity, that we learn one of the greatest truths life has to offer—adversity doesn't just shape us.—it reveals who is truly standing beside us.

When all is easy, when the table is full and the sun is shining, everyone wants a seat. Everyone wants to laugh with you, eat with you, and celebrate with you. But when the feast is gone, when the storms roll in, when your name isn't praised but questioned—watch closely. Watch who remains. Watch who tightens their grip on your hand rather than letting it slip away.

Adversity is the furnace that will cull the herd and burn off false friends. The pretenders, the impostors, the fair-weather companions—they cannot endure the heat. They wither. They make excuses. They disappear into the background like smoke caught in the wind. And you must let them. Because adversity is not taking anything from you. It is revealing to you with absolute clarity who belongs in your inner circle and who was only there for their own benefit.

We often make the mistake of thinking that loyalty is something we can see in easy times. We can't. True loyalty, true love, true brotherhood or sisterhood—they are invisible until pressure, pain, and fear pull back the curtains. Only when the music stops do you see who is truly dancing with you, not just to the sound of the song, but to the rhythm of your soul.

When your back is against the wall, real friends become a shield. Real friends become a voice when you have none, a light when you are lost, a fortress when you are attacked. And the false ones? They slip away into the night when you need them most. And good riddance. Because you don't need a crowd of bodies around you—you need a few loyal warriors who will fight for you when no one is watching.

Harsh conditions are a blessing in disguise. They prune your life. They make you lighter, sharper, stronger. The people who remain are not there because it benefits them—they are there because they believe in you. They see your worth when the world is blind to it. They lift you when you can't lift yourself. They remind you of who you are when the weight of the world tries to make you forget.

So, when you go through your valleys—when the storms rage, when you are broken, tired, bleeding—don't just cry about who left. Celebrate who stayed. Celebrate the few who leaned in closer when everyone else pulled away. These are your people. These are your tribe. They are worth more than a thousand casual acquaintances.

Remember this: life doesn't just test your strength. It tests your circle. It tests your relationships. It tests your alliances. And thank God it does, because we are not meant to carry dead weight into the battles we are called to fight or forced to endure.

In every trial, you are being refined—and so is your circle. Every hard moment is clarifying your path and your people. And the ones who make it through the fire with you? They are rare. They are precious. And they are enough.

So, when adversity comes, embrace it. If you listen, it will tell you the truth about the faces you see and the hands you hold. Adversity will sweep the stage clean so that only the real performers remain. And when the dust settles, you will stand, not alone, but surrounded by a few loyal souls who will walk through any fire with you. And that is worth more than gold.

Taking Action

Think | Write | Grow

Based on what you learned in this chapter:

What's something you will stop doing or a habit you will break?

_____

_____

What's something you will start doing or a habit you will create?

_____

_____

What's the potential positive impact of improving in this area?

_____

_____

Chapter Thirty-Three

Pain Is Lessened by Focusing on the Goal

Rival 5: Adversity

H ere is a profound insight worth remembering: Pain and discomfort diminish when we remain steadfastly focused on our goals. This principle, though simple in concept, holds immense power in practice.

Pain, whether physical or emotional, serves as both a warning signal and a powerful motivator. Pain can be a formidable distraction, diverting our attention from our dreams and aspirations, causing us to get off track and lose our focus. However, it can also alert us to potential harm, prompting immediate protective actions. The key lies in our response. Do we succumb to pain's distractions, or do we harness its energy to propel us forward?

Maintaining a clear focus on our objectives can significantly alter our perception of pain. When our minds are engrossed in a meaningful pursuit, discomfort often recedes into the background. This phenomenon is evident in various contexts. For instance, athletes often report diminished awareness of physical pain during intense competition, attributing this to their unwavering concentration on victory.

Neuroscientific research supports this experience. Studies show that attention and emotional states modulate pain perception. Focusing on a goal can activate neural pathways that diminish the intensity of pain signals, making discomfort more manageable. This underscores the profound connection between our mental focus and physical sensations.

Embracing discomfort as part of the journey can transform it into a source of motivation. Adopting a "no pain, no gain" mentality, when approached thoughtfully, can enhance our commitment to personal growth. By seeking challenges that push our boundaries, we cultivate resilience and foster a deeper sense of accomplishment.

To effectively manage pain and discomfort through goal-focused strategies, consider the following approaches:

1. Set Clear and Achievable Goals: Define your objectives with precision. Clear goals provide direction and purpose, making it easier to stay focused amidst challenges.

2. Break Goals Into Manageable Steps: Divide larger goals into smaller, actionable tasks. This approach prevents feelings of overwhelm and allows for steady progress, maintaining motivation.

3. Visualize Success: Regularly envision the successful attainment of your goals. Visualization reinforces commitment and can reduce the perceived intensity of obstacles.

4. Practice Consistent Mindfulness: Engage in mindfulness practices to enhance present-moment awareness. Mindfulness has been shown to reduce pain perception and improve focus.

5. Seek Support and Accountability: Share your goals with supportive and trusted individuals. External encouragement and accountability can bolster resilience during challenging times.

In essence, our perception of pain and discomfort is intricately linked to our mental focus. By steadfastly concentrating on our goals, we can diminish the impact of these sensations, transforming potential hindrances into catalysts for growth. Embrace challenges as integral components of your journey, and let your unwavering focus illuminate the path to success and motivate you to keep pressing forward.

Taking Action

Think | Write | Grow

Based on what you learned in this chapter:

What's something you will stop doing or a habit you will break?

_____

_____

What's something you will start doing or a habit you will create?

_____

_____

What's the potential positive impact of improving in this area?

_____

_____

Chapter Thirty-Four

Death Ground Enlists All Resources

Rival 5: Adversity

L et's explore a concept that has propelled individuals and organi- zations to remarkable achievements: the Death Ground Strategy. Originating from ancient military tactics, this strategy involves plac- ing oneself in a situation where retreat is impossible, thereby ignit- ing unparalleled determination and resourcefulness. By embracing such high-stakes scenarios, we unlock potential within ourselves that remains dormant in the comfort zones of life.

The term "Death Ground" traces back to the ancient Chinese military strategist Sun Tzu, who observed that soldiers fight with extraordinary vigor when their backs are against the wall and survival hinges on victory. In his seminal work, "The Art of War," Sun Tzu noted, "Throw your soldiers into positions whence there is no escape, and they will prefer death to flight." This principle underscores that when options are limited, commitment and performance reach their zenith.

History offers compelling examples of the Death Ground Strategy in action. In 1519, Spanish conquistador Hernán Cortés landed in Mexico with a mission to conquer the Aztec Empire. To eliminate any thought of retreat among his men, Cortés ordered the burning of their ships, leaving them no choice but to advance and succeed. This bold move exemplifies how eliminating escape routes can galvanize collective resolve and lead to monumental outcomes.

The efficacy of the Death Ground Strategy is deeply rooted in human psychology. When confronted with high-pressure situations where fail- ure is not an option, individuals often tap into reservoirs of creativity, focus, and resilience previously unexplored. This heightened state of urgency compels us to transcend perceived limitations and achieve feats that might otherwise seem unattainable.

While the Death Ground Strategy originates from military doctrine, its principles profoundly apply to contemporary personal and professional settings. Entrepreneurs often embody this strategy when they invest their life savings into a venture, knowing that success is imperative for financial survival. Professionals may place themselves on death ground by accepting challenging assignments beyond their capabilities. Individuals striving for significant lifestyle changes, such as overcoming addictions or achieving fitness goals, might create environments where reverting to old habits is not an option, thus enforcing discipline and commitment.

To effectively harness the power of the Death Ground Strategy, eliminate safety nets, set ambitious deadlines, create high-stakes scenarios, and cultivate a do-or-die mindset. While this strategy can be a powerful catalyst for action, it is essential to apply it judiciously by assessing risks, adequately preparing, and maintaining ethical standards by avoiding compromising the principles or well-being of others.

Choosing to put yourself in a death ground scenario involves a deliberate choice to step beyond the boundaries of comfort and security, entering arenas where only unwavering commitment and relentless effort can secure success. By doing so, we enlist all resources, awaken latent potentials, foster resilience, and position ourselves to achieve extraordinary outcomes. As we navigate the complexities of modern life, let us remember that, sometimes, the most profound growth emerges when we stand with our backs against the wall, compelled to fight not just for survival, but for the realization of our greatest aspirations.

Taking Action

Think | Write | Grow

Based on what you learned in this chapter:

What's something you will stop doing or a habit you will break?

_____

_____

What's something you will start doing or a habit you will create?

_____

_____

What's the potential positive impact of improving in this area?

_____

_____

Chapter Thirty-Five

Scars Prove That Wounds Have Healed

Rival 5: Adversity

Scars aren't just physical—they can be emotional, mental, and spiritual as well. The scars we carry, physically or metaphorically, are tangible evidence that our wounds have healed, and they stand as enduring symbols of our strength and resilience. Each scar, whether visible on our skin or etched within our hearts, tells a story of survival, growth, and the indomitable human spirit.

A scar forms when the body repairs tissue damage, replacing normal skin with fibrous tissue. This natural healing process signifies a wound has closed, and the body has mended itself. Beyond their physical manifestation, scars embody our journey through pain and recovery, serving as permanent reminders of our capacity to heal and continue pressing forward.

Our scars are not merely blemishes—they are badges of honor that showcase our resilience. They remind us that we have faced adversity and emerged stronger. Our scars offer irrefutable proof that we are stronger than who or what tried to hurt us. Each scar signifies a battle fought and won, highlighting our ability to overcome challenges.

Embracing our scars involves acknowledging our past without allowing it to define us. It means accepting that, while we cannot change what happened, we can choose how we perceive and respond to it. This perspective empowers us to take control of our narrative, transforming marks of pain into symbols of survival. As highlighted in a reflection on healing and resilience, "We all wear scars, but it is how we choose to view them that matters."

The Japanese art of Kintsugi offers a profound metaphor for embracing our scars. This technique involves repairing broken pottery with lacquer mixed with powdered gold, silver, or platinum, treating breakage and repair as part of the object's history rather than something to disguise. Similarly, our scars add to our unique beauty and character, reminding us that healing can render us more beautiful and resilient than before.

Our scars also serve as bridges to others, fostering empathy and connection. When we openly share our struggles and the lessons we've learned, we create opportunities for support and understanding. This vulnerability strengthens our relationships, encouraging others to share their own stories and reinforcing our shared humanity. Some of the strongest relationships that exist between two people have been forged in the fire of the scars they share.

Our scars can catalyze personal growth, transforming our pain into purpose. By reflecting on our experiences, we can derive valuable lessons that shape our character and guide our future actions. This transformation allows us to use our past challenges as fuel for positive change, both in our lives and in the lives of others.

Our scars are not merely remnants of past wounds but powerful symbols of healing, strength, and resilience. They testify to our ability to endure hardship and emerge stronger, embodying our journey toward wholeness. By embracing our scars, we honor our experiences, foster deeper connections with others, and transform our pain into purpose. Let us wear our scars with pride, acknowledging them as integral parts of our unique stories and as emblems of the strength that lies within us. After all, it is the injuries that you have endured and survived that have molded your fortitude and shaped your resilience—so don't cover them—embrace them!

Taking Action

Think | Write | Grow

Based on what you learned in this chapter:

What's something you will stop doing or a habit you will break?

_____

_____

What's something you will start doing or a habit you will create?

_____

_____

What's the potential positive impact of improving in this area?

_____

_____

RIVAL 6

D I S T R A C T I O N S

"Focus On Growth"

Chapter Thirty-Six

Procrastination Is Overt Self-Sabotage

Rival 6: Distractions

We all have dreams. Most have goals. But many of us fall into a silent, persistent trap that keeps us from reaching them. That trap is called procrastination—and make no mistake, it's not just a bad habit. It's a quiet, insidious form of self-sabotage.

You see, procrastination isn't just about putting things off. It's about putting off *yourself*. It's delaying your future. It's postponing your potential. It's telling your dreams, "Not today," again and again until "someday" turns into *never*.

Let's call it what it is—it's a defense mechanism. Procrastination often disguises itself as perfectionism or a need for more time or energy. But underneath all those excuses is fear—fear of failure, fear of judgment, and fear of success. And instead of confronting that fear, we distract ourselves. We delay. We scroll. We say, "I'll start tomorrow," even when we know that tomorrow is never guaranteed.

Think about the opportunities you've missed not because you weren't good enough—but because you didn't show up. Think about the goals you've set, written down, talked about—but never acted on. Now ask yourself: Was the problem the goal? Or was it your inaction?

The cold, hard truth is that success is rarely about brilliance. It's not just for the most talented, the most educated, or the most connected. It's for the most disciplined. It's for the people who act despite the fear, who start even when they're not ready, who take small steps every single day.

Procrastination stops momentum before it can take its first step. It convinces you that waiting is safer than failing. But the real danger isn't failure—it's standing still. It's letting time slip away while you wait for the "perfect" moment that will never come. Every time you procrastinate, you send a message to yourself that says, "This goal isn't important enough for me to prioritize it." You say, "I don't believe in my ability to do this." You reinforce doubt instead of confidence. You choose comfort over courage.

But you have a choice. You can choose to act. You can choose to fight back against the voice that says, "Not yet." You can take the small but important steps that build momentum. Start small. One task. One hour. One decision. The more you act, the more capable you feel. The more capable you feel, the more you do. And before you know it, you've replaced delay with discipline.

Look at any high achiever—athletes, entrepreneurs, artists. They didn't get where they are because they waited until they felt inspired. They got there because they worked when they were tired or when they had zero motivation. They trained when it was inconvenient. They acted when no one was watching. They built productive habits that overpowered their hesitations.

So, I challenge you. Stop waiting for the mood to strike, for the fear to disappear, for the right time to present itself. The right time is now. This moment. This decision. This choice. Your goals are waiting for you—but they won't wait forever. The longer you put things off, the more distant your dreams become. And the only way to close that gap is through consistent, courageous action.

Let this be your turning point. Let today be the day you stop self-sabotaging and start self-building. The day you go from wishing to working. The day you stop procrastinating on your potential and start becoming who you were always meant to be. The clock is ticking. Success isn't patient, and when it knocks on your door, neither should you be. Say no to the distractions and excuses, and take action now!

Taking Action

Think | Write | Grow

Based on what you learned in this chapter:

What's something you will stop doing or a habit you will break?

_____

_____

What's something you will start doing or a habit you will create?

_____

_____

What's the potential positive impact of improving in this area?

_____

_____

Chapter Thirty-Seven

Success Requires Successful Habits

Rival 6: Distractions

I f you want to change your life, don't start with your goals—start with your habits. Goals are where we want to go, but habits are the vehicle that gets us there. Your future isn't shaped by one massive decision—it's shaped by the small things you choose to do every single day. Productive habits are the foundation of success.

Whether you want to improve your health, grow your business, build a skill, or reach personal milestones, it all starts with what you repeatedly do. The most successful people in the world aren't always the most talented, but they are often the most consistent. And consistency is born from strong habits.

Let's be honest—bad habits are easy. They require little to no effort. It's easy to procrastinate. It's easy to stay up late. It's easy to avoid the hard things. But easy now means hard later. And hard now means easy later. That's the power of habits. They either work for you, or they work against you. So, how do we create a new routine that serves our dreams instead of sabotaging them?

Here are five steps to build productive habits that stick:

Start Small: You don't have to overhaul your life overnight. That's a recipe for burnout. Instead, focus on one habit at a time. Want to start reading more? Start with 5 pages a day. Want to exercise regularly? Begin with 10 minutes a day. Small wins create momentum, and momentum creates transformation.

Make It Obvious: Design your environment to support your new habit. Want to eat healthier? Keep fruits and vegetables on the counter instead of chips. Want to journal daily? Keep a notebook by your bed. The easier you make it to start a habit, the more likely it is to stick.

Link It to an Existing Routine: Pair your new habit with something you already do. This is called habit stacking. For example, "After I brush my teeth, I'll write down one thing I'm grateful for." This creates a natural trigger and makes the habit part of your existing routine.

Track Your Progress: There's something powerful about seeing a streak. Use a calendar, app, or journal to track your habits. It gives you a visual reminder of your consistency—and you'll find yourself wanting to keep that streak alive.

Be Patient and Persistent: Habits aren't built in a day. They're built through repetition. There will be days you miss, days you don't feel like it, days when life gets in the way. But success doesn't come from perfection—it comes from persistence. Miss a day? Fine. Just don't miss two. Get back on track and keep moving forward.

Productive habits don't just make you more efficient—they change how you see yourself. Every time you follow through, you reinforce the belief that you are someone who follows through. You become someone who values growth, who chooses progress, who takes control of their time and energy. You don't rise to the level of your goals—you fall to the level of your routines, so build routines that serve you and pull you toward the life you want.

Taking Action

Think | Write | Grow

Based on what you learned in this chapter:

What's something you will stop doing or a habit you will break?

_____

_____

What's something you will start doing or a habit you will create?

_____

_____

What's the potential positive impact of improving in this area?

_____

_____

Chapter Thirty-Eight

Habits Are the Manifestation of Beliefs

Rival 6: Distractions

Beliefs lie beneath the surface of our daily routines, meaning the habits we form are not random acts, but powerful manifestations of what we truly believe about ourselves and the world around us. Every time you repeat a habit—whether it's waking up early to work out or hitting the snooze button, choosing to read a book or scrolling endlessly through your phone—you are casting a vote. A vote for the kind of person you believe yourself to be. Habits are not just what we do. They are reflections of who we believe we are.

If you believe you're a healthy person, you don't have to force yourself to eat better or exercise—you do it because it aligns with who you see yourself as. If you believe you're disciplined, you don't need to be constantly motivated to work—you work because it's part of your identity. But if deep down you believe you're lazy, unworthy, or incapable, your habits will reflect that, too.

So many people try to change their lives by focusing only on the actions—waking up earlier, working harder, eating better. But lasting change doesn't come from the outside in. It comes from the inside out. Your habits are the mirror of your mindset. If you want to change your behavior, start by changing your beliefs. If you want to build better habits, start by believing something better about yourself.

A person who smokes doesn't quit by just saying, "I'm trying to quit." The real change happens when they say, "I'm not a smoker anymore." That belief shift drives the new behavior. Identity always leads our actions. So, what do your current habits say about what you believe? Do you stay up late watching TV because, deep down, you believe you'll never get ahead anyway, so what's the point in trying harder? Do you skip workouts or projects because you don't truly believe you're capable of change, or worthy of success? Do you procrastinate because you fear failure, and that fear is rooted in the belief that you're not enough?

It's time to flip the script. What if you believed you were enough? What if you believed you were capable? What if you believed you were worthy of health, happiness, purpose, and success? Your habits would begin to change. Not out of guilt or pressure, but out of alignment with a new identity. You can't outperform the beliefs you hold about yourself.

If you want to grow, you have to build new beliefs—and then prove them to yourself through small, consistent action. Don't wait until you feel like you're that person. Start acting like them now. Confidence doesn't come from perfection. It comes from evidence that you perceive as truth. So, start giving yourself evidence.

If you want to believe you're disciplined, start showing up. Even when it's hard. If you want to believe you're healthy, make one better choice today. If you want to believe you're a leader, start leading—even if no one's following yet. And as those small actions compound, they'll reinforce the belief that you are becoming exactly who you're meant to be. In the end, your habits will either confirm your old limits or help you build new possibilities.

So I challenge you to not just try to change what you do—change what you believe. And let those beliefs become the foundation for powerful, intentional, life-changing habits. Because once you believe it's possible… you'll act like it's possible. And once you act like it's possible, it becomes your new reality.

Taking Action

Think | Write | Grow

Based on what you learned in this chapter:

What's something you will stop doing or a habit you will break?

_____

_____

What's something you will start doing or a habit you will create?

_____

_____

What's the potential positive impact of improving in this area?

_____

_____

Chapter Thirty-Nine

The Pain Of Self-Discipline Is Temporary

Rival 6: Distractions

Let's talk about two kinds of pain. One is sharp but short-lived. The other is dull but relentless. One builds you up, while the other breaks you down. One strengthens your character, while the other steals your peace. I'm talking about the pain of self-discipline and the pain of regret. The pain of self-discipline is temporary, but the pain of regret lasts forever.

Self-discipline hurts, doesn't it? Waking up early when you'd rather sleep. Saying no to distractions when everyone else is giving in. Choosing the hard path when the easy one is right in front of you. Discipline demands sacrifice. It asks for your time, your energy, your comfort. And, in the moment, it can feel like a burden. But here's what makes discipline different from regret—it has a purpose. Discipline is pain with a payoff. It's the struggle that leads to strength. It's the discomfort that leads to growth. It's the price you pay now to avoid a much greater cost later. Because regret is a thief.

Regret doesn't show up immediately. It's quiet at first. It waits. It lets you enjoy the moment of procrastination, the moment of laziness, the moment of giving in. And then it hits you right between the eyes when it's too late to do anything about it. It shows up when the opportunity has passed. When the deadline has expired. When the moment is gone and can't be reclaimed. That's the kind of pain that lingers. The kind that keeps you awake at night. The kind that whispers, "If only you had tried harder. If only you had shown up. If only you had been disciplined when it mattered."

Every time you choose comfort over commitment, you're choosing regret over results. But the beautiful thing is—you have a choice. Discipline hurts, but only for a little while. That 5 a.m. workout may be uncomfortable, but it's done in an hour—and the pride lasts all day. That hour of focused work may require focus and energy, but it moves you closer to your goals. That choice to say no to something unhealthy or unproductive may feel hard now—but you'll thank yourself tomorrow, next week, next year. Every disciplined decision is a deposit into your future. Every sacrifice today creates a reward down the road. And the more you train yourself to endure the temporary pain of discipline, the less you will ever have to suffer the endless ache of regret.

Discipline is not about perfection. It's about progress. It's about showing up even when you don't feel like it. It's about choosing your future over your feelings. It's not always easy—but it is always worth it. You will never regret being disciplined. You will never regret giving your best effort. You will never regret doing the right thing, the hard thing, the thing that stretched you and strengthened you. But you will regret quitting. You will regret watching the clock tick by while your dreams gather dust.

So, I ask you, what pain are you willing to live with? The pain of discipline that leads to strength, success, and self-respect? Or the pain of regret that follows you and reminds you of what could have been? Choose discipline. Choose discomfort now so you can enjoy freedom later. Choose the pain that pays off, not the pain that wears you down. And when it gets hard—when you want to quit—remember this: Discipline weighs an ounce, but regret weighs a ton. So, pick up the weight of discipline and carry it with resolve and tenacity, because it is the key ingredient to the life you want.

Taking Action

Think | Write | Grow

Based on what you learned in this chapter:

What's something you will stop doing or a habit you will break?

_____

_____

What's something you will start doing or a habit you will create?

_____

_____

What's the potential positive impact of improving in this area?

_____

_____

Chapter Forty

Perfectionism is the Enemy of Productivity

Rival 6: Distractions

How many dreams have died at the hands of perfectionism? How many brilliant ideas, projects, and passions have been delayed, derailed, or destroyed—not because they weren't good enough, but because they weren't perfect?

Perfectionism is one of the most subtle, yet most dangerous, enemies of productivity and achievement. It doesn't show up with a warning sign. It doesn't scream, "I'm here to stop your progress." Instead, it whispers, "It's not ready yet." "It's not good enough." "You're not good enough." And so, you wait. You tweak. You hesitate. You delay. Until one day, you realize that time has passed, momentum has faded, and that spark you once had has gone cold.

Perfectionism is not the pursuit of excellence. Excellence is about doing your best—perfectionism is about being afraid your best won't be enough. It's fear wearing a disguise. Fear of judgment. Fear of failure. Fear of not being accepted or approved. And because of that fear, perfectionism convinces us to do nothing at all unless we can do it perfectly. But the fact of the matter is, "Done is better than perfect."

Perfectionism kills momentum, paralyzes progress, and steals the one thing we can never get back, which is time. While you wait for the perfect plan, someone else is out there taking imperfect action—and they're learning, growing, and moving forward while you're stuck in neutral. How many times have you stopped yourself from starting something because you didn't feel ready? How many times have you told yourself, "I'll start when I have more time, more knowledge, more confidence"?

That's perfectionism. That's the illusion that everything needs to align before you begin.

Success doesn't come to those who wait for perfect conditions. Success comes to those who take action, learn as they go, and adjust along the way. Action creates clarity. Perfectionism only creates procrastination. Think about the fact that the first draft of a bestselling book is usually messy. The first version of a hit product isn't flawless—it's functional. The most successful people didn't wait until they had every answer. They started, they stumbled, they failed, and they improved. Progress beats perfection, always!

So, how do we defeat perfectionism?

First, accept that mistakes are part of the process. They are not signs of weakness, but proof that you're moving forward. Every misstep is a lesson. Every setback is a setup for a comeback.

Second, set realistic expectations. Instead of aiming for perfect, aim for progress. Instead of asking, "Is this flawless?" Ask, "Is this moving me closer to my goal?"

Third, take action. Even if it's messy. Even if it's uncomfortable. Perfectionism hates movement—so get in motion. Start small. Start simple. Just start.

Finally, give yourself permission to grow. You are a work in progress, not a finished product. Your effort matters more than your polish. Your courage matters more than your image. And your willingness to show up—even imperfectly—is the most powerful step you can take.

Perfection is the enemy of done. The enemy of started. The enemy of achieved. Let go of the need to impress. Let go of the fear of judgment. Let go of the lie that you need to be flawless to be worthy. You don't. You are enough right now—right here—to begin. To try. To create. To contribute. So show up, speak up, and put your work out there because while perfectionism wants you to keep polishing, your future self is waiting for your progress.

Taking Action

Think | Write | Grow

Based on what you learned in this chapter:

What's something you will stop doing or a habit you will break?

_____

_____

What's something you will start doing or a habit you will create?

_____

_____

What's the potential positive impact of improving in this area?

_____

_____

Chapter Forty-One

Healthy Relationships Respect Boundaries

Rival 6: Distractions

S etting boundaries isn't selfish. It isn't rude. And it isn't a sign of weakness. Setting boundaries is a form of self-care, self-respect, and emotional strength. So many of us go through life trying to be everything to everyone. We say yes when we want to say no. We stretch ourselves thin trying to meet expectations that aren't ours. We pour into others until we're empty, then wonder why we feel burned out, resentful, and disconnected.

Let me say this loud and clear—you are allowed to protect your peace. You are allowed to say, "This doesn't work for me." You are allowed to walk away from what drains you and lean into what energizes you. Setting boundaries is not about building walls to shut people out. It's about creating space to honor your own needs so that you can show up for life—not depleted, but empowered.

Visualize boundaries as the fences that protect your garden. You don't build a fence because you hate what's outside—you build it because you value what's inside. And healthy relationships will value what's inside, too. People who truly care about you will not punish you for protecting your peace. They won't shame you for needing space. They won't guilt you for saying no. They won't take offense when you express your limits with honesty and grace.

If someone resents your boundaries, it's not a reflection of your failure—it's a reflection of their comfort with taking advantage of your silence or ignoring your wishes. Respect is the foundation of every strong relationship—personal or professional. And when you establish boundaries, you're not just standing up for yourself, you're raising the standard for how you will be treated.

Setting boundaries isn't always easy. Especially if you're used to people-pleasing and if you've been taught to equate self-worth with self-sacrifice. But trust me—the discomfort of disappointing others is nothing compared to the damage of constantly disappointing yourself. And the beautiful part is that when you set boundaries, you invite in people who respect your values, who honor your time, and who love you with no need to control or consume you. You attract relationships rooted in authenticity, not obligation. Boundaries teach people how to treat you. And, more importantly, they teach *you* how to treat yourself.

So, if you struggle with setting boundaries—start small. Say no without apologizing. End conversations that feel toxic. Take time for yourself without explaining why. Let go of relationships that only thrive when you're giving more than you can afford. It's not your job to carry everyone. It's your job to carry yourself with dignity.

In the end, setting boundaries isn't about closing off your heart. It's about opening your life to peace, clarity, and genuine connection. It's about knowing that your needs matter, your time is valuable, and your well-being is worth protecting. So protect it. Honor it. Stand by it because you don't have to burn out to be worthy, you don't have to say yes to be loved, and you don't have to be everything to everyone to be enough. You are already enough, just as you are, and your established and protected boundaries are proof that you believe it.

Taking Action

Think | Write | Grow

Based on what you learned in this chapter:

What's something you will stop doing or a habit you will break?

_____

_____

What's something you will start doing or a habit you will create?

_____

_____

What's the potential positive impact of improving in this area?

_____

_____

Chapter Forty-Two

Focus Is the Art of Knowing What to Ignore

Rival 6: Distractions

I n a world full of noise, distractions, and constant demands on our attention, there is one skill that has become more powerful than ever—focus. Focus is not just about paying attention, it's about choosing what *not* to pay attention to. It's the art of knowing what to ignore, and in that choice lies the foundation of true productivity, creativity, and success.

We live in a time where it's easy to be busy but not productive. We're constantly checking emails, replying to messages, switching between apps, and juggling endless tasks—all while telling ourselves we're "getting things done." But the truth is, productivity isn't about doing more—it's about doing what matters most. And to do what matters most, you have to be able to say "no" to what doesn't.

That's where focus comes in. It's a decision muscle that needs to be trained. It's the discipline to tune out the noise and lock into your mission. It's knowing that you don't need to chase every opportunity—just the right ones. That you don't need to respond to every notification—just the ones that move your goals forward. Success doesn't belong to the most talented, the most popular, or the most connected. It belongs to the most focused.

A magnifying glass can take the power of sunlight and start a fire—but only when it focuses all that energy on one point. The same is true for you. When your energy, attention, and effort are scattered, your results will be, too. But when you narrow your focus, you ignite progress. Focus helps you eliminate the unnecessary so you can concentrate on the essential. It helps you work with clarity instead of chaos. With intention, instead of reaction.

Focus doesn't mean your journey will be easy. In fact, distractions will try harder than ever to steal your attention. The world will pull at you from every angle—social media, emails, drama, doubts, even your own inner critic. But your job is to ask yourself one powerful question every single day: What matters most right now? And then protect your focus like your life depends on it—because, in a way, it does.

Focus is what allows you to build momentum. It's what helps you finish what you start. It's what separates dreams from execution. Without focus, you'll chase everything—and achieve nothing. Steve Jobs once said, "People think focus means saying yes to the thing you've got to focus on. But that's not what it means. It means saying no to the hundred other good ideas that there are." That's not just advice—that's a blueprint.

To develop focus in a distracted world, know your priorities, create a distraction-free environment, work in blocks, and get into the habit of saying no more often. Focus is not about being rigid. It's about being resilient. It's the quiet force that helps you tune out the noise and lock in on your purpose. And when you do that—day after day—you will begin to see extraordinary results from ordinary actions.

I challenge you to ask yourself: What am I willing to ignore so I can give my best to what truly matters? Because the future belongs to those who can focus. Not on everything, just on what counts.

Taking Action

Think | Write | Grow

Based on what you learned in this chapter:

What's something you will stop doing or a habit you will break?

_____

_____

What's something you will start doing or a habit you will create?

_____

_____

What's the potential positive impact of improving in this area?

_____

_____

RIVAL 7

M I N D S E T

"Shatter Your Limits"

Chapter Forty-Three

Our Experiences Produce Our Attitudes

Rival 7: Mindset

Our attitude is one of the most powerful forces in our lives. It influences how we see the world, how we react to challenges, how we treat others, and how we pursue our goals. Attitude is the lens through which we view everything—and that lens can either blur our vision or sharpen our focus. But the good news is that attitudes are not fixed—they are formed, and they can be changed.

Let's start with how attitudes are created. They aren't born with us. No one comes into this world with a built-in attitude. Instead, our attitudes are shaped over time—by our environment, our experiences, our upbringing, and the voices we choose to listen to. If you grow up around negativity, criticism, and fear, chances are you'll start to view the world through a similar lens. If you're constantly told that you're not good enough, that the world is unfair, or that failure is final, those thoughts can settle into your mind and become your attitude. But if you've experienced encouragement, support, and resilience, you're more likely to develop an optimistic, hopeful, and determined outlook. Why? Because attitude is a habit of thought. And like any habit—it can be broken, and it can be rebuilt.

The problem is, most people think their attitude is just "how they are." But the truth is, your attitude is how you choose to be. And yes, it *is* a choice. You may not be able to control every circumstance in your life. You may not get to choose the setbacks, the disappointments, or the challenges. But you always have a choice in how you respond to them. You can choose bitterness, or you can choose growth. You can choose blame, or you can choose responsibility. You can choose fear, or you can choose faith.

Every moment is a decision point. So, how do we change our attitude? How do we shift the internal narrative when life feels overwhelming, unfair, or just plain hard?

First, you must become aware of your current attitude. Pay attention to how you speak to yourself and to others. Are your thoughts filled with possibility—or with doubt? Are you expecting the best—or bracing for the worst? You can't change what you're not aware of.

Second, change the input. Garbage in, garbage out. If you want to elevate your attitude, you have to upgrade your environment. Read books that inspire you. Listen to uplifting messages. Surround yourself with people who challenge you to rise, not shrink.

Third, practice gratitude. Nothing shifts your attitude faster than recognizing what you already have. Gratitude turns what you have into enough—and it transforms your outlook from scarcity to abundance.

Fourth, take action. Sometimes the best way to change your attitude is to change your behavior. Do something productive. Serve someone else. Make progress, even if it's small. Motion creates emotion. When you act positively, even when you don't feel like it, your attitude begins to follow.

And finally, repeat. Just like any habit, a positive attitude takes practice. Daily repetition. Constant correction. But over time, it becomes who you are—not because you were born that way, but because you built it that way.

If you identify a destructive habit, change it. You are not stuck with the attitudes of yesterday. You are not defined by the negativity of your past. You are the author of your perspective, and your perspective is the foundation of your power. Your attitude is your choice, so choose hope, choose faith, choose strength, and choose growth. When you change your attitude, you change your world.

Taking Action

Think | Write | Grow

Based on what you learned in this chapter:

What's something you will stop doing or a habit you will break?

_____

_____

What's something you will start doing or a habit you will create?

_____

_____

What's the potential positive impact of improving in this area?

_____

_____

Chapter Forty-Four

Biases Affect How We Think and Act

Rival 7: Mindset

B iases are those invisible beliefs we carry, often without realizing it, that shape how we see the world, how we see others, and how we see ourselves. Biases aren't just opinions—they're mental short-cuts—built from our experiences, upbringing, media, and culture. They influence our decisions, actions, and interactions. And while some biases help us make quick decisions, many of them block us from the very things we're working so hard to achieve.

Let's expose some of the most common biases that are standing between us and the life we truly want—and learn how to rise above them.

First is "Confirmation Bias," which is the need to be right. We all love being right. So much so that we seek out information that confirms what we already believe—and ignore anything that challenges it. In our careers, this stops us from learning. It keeps us stuck in the same thinking that created our problems in the first place. In our relation-ships, it causes us to judge others unfairly or shut down conversations that could bring understanding. Solution? Stay curious. Ask yourself: What if I'm wrong? Growth begins where certainty ends.

Second is "Negativity Bias," which focuses on the worst. Have you ever noticed how you can receive 10 compliments but obsess over one criticism? That's negativity bias—our brain's tendency to focus more on bad experiences than good ones. This bias robs us of joy. It keeps us dwelling on past mistakes, fearing failure, and second-guessing our decisions. It holds us back from taking risks and celebrating progress. Solution? Practice gratitude. Train your mind to notice what's working, not just what's broken. The more you focus on the positive, the more confident and courageous you become.

Third is "Impostor Bias," which is the lie of not being enough. So many people walk through life feeling like frauds, believing they don't deserve their success or that they'll be "found out." This is a form of self-bias that says, "I'm not good enough," even in the face of evidence to the contrary. It leads to self-sabotage. It prevents us from speaking up, applying for that promotion, or stepping into leadership. Solution? Remind yourself that you don't have to feel confident to take action. Repetitive action builds confidence and belief. Show up, even if don't feel you're worthy. That's how self-trust is born.

Fourth is "Halo Effect Bias," which is judging the book by one chapter. We often let one good impression—or one bad one—color our entire opinion of a person. This is called the halo effect. It causes us to overvalue certain traits and overlook flaws, or vice versa. In relationships, this bias leads to unrealistic expectations or unfair judgments. In teams, it prevents us from seeing the full potential of others—or ourselves. Solution? Slow down. See the whole person. One moment doesn't define someone's character. Give people ample time to show you their true selves before making final decisions.

Fifth is "Availability Bias," which is believing what is easiest to recall. If something is recent, dramatic, or emotionally charged, we tend to give it more weight than it deserves. That's availability bias. It's why we fear rare things and underestimate everyday risks. It's why one bad experience with someone can ruin our trust in many. It leads to assumptions that keep us from taking action or building meaningful connections. Solution? Don't let loud thoughts speak as truth. Check the facts. Ask for context. Let reason guide you, not just memory.

These biases aren't signs of failure—they're signs that you're human. But being human also means having the power to grow, to reflect, and to choose better thoughts. Remember that your future success can be blocked by your assumptions. Question your patterns, challenge your assumptions, and give yourself and others the grace to grow.

Taking Action

Think | Write | Grow

Based on what you learned in this chapter:

What's something you will stop doing or a habit you will break?

_____

_____

What's something you will start doing or a habit you will create?

_____

_____

What's the potential positive impact of improving in this area?

_____

_____

Chapter Forty-Five

Perspective Is Our Greatest Superpower

Rival 7: Mindset

I f I told you that you had a superpower—one that could change your life instantly—would you believe me? A power that could turn failure into fuel, problems into possibilities, and setbacks into stepping stones? That power isn't money, talent, or connections. It's something far more accessible. That power is called perspective. Perspective is how we choose to see the world. It's the lens through which we interpret every situation, every challenge, every success, and every failure. And the most exciting thing about perspective is that you can change it in the blink of an eye.

Your circumstances don't have to change for your life to change—your perspective does. Two people can face the same obstacle. One sees defeat, the other sees opportunity. One gives up, the other grows. Why? Because their perspectives are different. Your perspective determines your mindset, your mindset shapes your actions, and your actions, repeated over time, create your reality. Put simply, how you choose to see things has a significant impact on how you experience them. Think about it. You can see a Monday morning as the worst day of the week—or as a brand-new beginning. You can see a difficult person as a problem—or as a teacher, pushing you to grow in patience and self-control. You can see a failure as proof that you're not good enough—or as evidence that you were brave enough to try. It's not about what happens to you—it's about how you choose to frame what happens to you.

Here's the good news—you are not stuck with the perspective you woke up with. You can shift it at any moment. You can choose a different thought. You can decide to interpret things differently. That is your superpower. And unlike superpowers in the movies—you don't have to

179

be bitten by a radioactive spider or travel to another planet to unlock it. You already have it. But, like any power, it requires awareness, intention, and effort.

So, how do you shift your perspective when life feels heavy, when challenges feel overwhelming, when doubt creeps in? Let me give you three simple tools.

First, ask better questions. Your mind is always searching for answers. So, feed it empowering questions. Instead of asking, "Why is this happening to me?" Ask, "What is this teaching me?" Instead of "What if I fail?" Ask, "What if I grow?" The questions you ask shape the perspective you choose.

Second, step outside the frame. Sometimes we get stuck because we're too close to the situation. We're living inside the frame—so all we can see is the problem. But when you step back—when you zoom out—you see things differently. Talk to someone you trust. Take a walk. Journal your thoughts. Get outside of your own head. Perspective expands when we change our vantage point.

Third, practice gratitude. Gratitude is the ultimate perspective shift. It doesn't erase your challenges—but it reminds you of what's still good, what's still working, and what's still worth fighting for. When you focus on what you have, rather than what you lack, your entire mindset shifts from scarcity to abundance, from stress to strength.

Shifting your perspective doesn't mean denying reality. It means deciding to focus on the potential for gain or growth instead of the negatives. The most successful people in the world aren't those who avoid adversity—they're the ones who use perspective to turn adversity into advantage. They've trained themselves to see the light during dark moments or events. And that ability—that superpower—is available to you.

So, the next time you feel stuck, overwhelmed, or discouraged, remember: you don't have to change the circumstances, you just need to leverage the power of perspective. Use it wisely and boldly to build the life that you want.

Taking Action

Think | Write | Grow

Based on what you learned in this chapter:

What's something you will stop doing or a habit you will break?

_____

_____

What's something you will start doing or a habit you will create?

_____

_____

What's the potential positive impact of improving in this area?

_____

_____

Chapter Forty-Six

Time, Energy, and Mindset are Treasures

Rival 7: Mindset

T here is a simple truth that is often forgotten in the chaos of life, which is that you are the gatekeeper of your time, your energy, and your mindset. And in a world that is constantly pulling at you from every direction, learning to protect these three things isn't just important—it's essential.

Let's start with time. Time is the most valuable resource you have. It's not renewable. You can't earn more of it. You can't get it back once it's gone. And yet, how often do we give it away so easily—to distractions, to obligations that don't align with our purpose, to people who drain us instead of building us? Every minute you spend is an investment. And you need to ask yourself daily: Is this investment bringing me closer to who or where I want to be? Because if it isn't, it's time to set some boundaries. Busyness is not a badge of honor. Being overwhelmed is not a sign of importance. What matters is being intentional with your calendar, your commitments, and menial distractions. Every time you say "yes" to something that doesn't matter, you are saying "no" to something that does.

Now let's talk about energy. You are not a machine. You can't pour from an empty cup. If you are constantly giving without refueling, constantly doing without resting, constantly serving others while neglecting yourself—you will burn out. And when you burn out, the very people you want to help and the goals you want to reach suffer as a result. Protecting your energy means knowing what recharges you—and making it a priority. That might be solitude. It might be movement. It might be prayer, meditation, or a meaningful connection. Whatever it is, treat it like oxygen. Because without it, everything else begins to suffocate.

Lastly, let's talk about mindset. Your mindset is your internal operating system. It determines how you see the world, how you respond to challenges, and how you view yourself. A strong mindset turns set-backs into comebacks. A strong mindset sees rejection as redirection. A strong mindset doesn't ask, "Why me?" but says, "Try me." But here's the thing—your mindset must be guarded. Negative voices, toxic environments, limiting beliefs—they're like weeds. If you're not actively pulling them out and planting positive seeds, they'll overtake your mental garden. So ask yourself: What are you feeding your mind? Are you surrounding yourself with people who inspire, or people who drain? Are you consuming content that empowers, or content that numbs? Are your thoughts building you up or tearing you down? You become what you allow, what you tolerate, and what you focus on.

If you want to build a meaningful life—if you want to reach the next level—you must protect your time, your energy, and your mindset like your dreams depend on it, because they do. That might mean having hard conversations or stepping away from people or situations that no longer serve your growth. That might mean learning to say "no" without guilt and "yes" to yourself without apology. It's not selfish—it's self-respect and self-care.

You are not here to be everything to everyone. You are here to live a life of purpose, joy, and impact. But to do that, you need the clarity that comes from a protected mind, the strength that comes from protected energy, and the direction that comes from protected time. Guard your time like it's gold. Guard your energy like it's sacred. Guard your mindset like it's your lifeline—because it is. Fiercely and diligently protect what matters most, and prioritize what fuels you, and watch your life transform.

Taking Action

Think | Write | Grow

Based on what you learned in this chapter:

What's something you will stop doing or a habit you will break?

_____

_____

What's something you will start doing or a habit you will create?

_____

_____

What's the potential positive impact of improving in this area?

_____

_____

Chapter Forty-Seven

Mindset Requires Attitudes to Be Aligned

Rival 7: Mindset

I f there's one thing that determines whether you rise or fall, grow or stay stuck, push forward or give up—it's your mindset. Mindset isn't just a buzzword. It's not just thinking positively or "keeping your chin up." Mindset is much deeper than that. It is the foundation of how you interpret the world, how you respond to challenges, and how you pursue your goals. It is the alignment of all your attitudes working in the same direction—toward your vision, your purpose, your passion.

Your mindset comprises the attitudes you carry about life, about people, and most importantly—about yourself. And just like a car won't move forward efficiently if its wheels are misaligned, you won't move toward your goals unless your thoughts, beliefs, and emotions are aligned and working together in harmony. That means if you say you want a promotion at your job but you have a poor work ethic, you are out of alignment. If you say you want love, but your attitude toward vulnerability is fear, you are out of alignment. If you say you want growth, but your attitude toward failure is avoidance, you are out of alignment.

This is why so many people set goals every year and never reach them. It's not because they don't want it badly enough. It's because their attitudes are working against their intentions. Your mindset is not just about what you *wish* for—it's about what you're *committed* to. It's about making sure your internal compass is pointed in the right direction, so when the hard days come—and they will—you don't fall apart or fall behind.

So, how do you align your attitudes with your goals? How do you build a mindset that's unshakable? Here are three key steps:

First, examine your beliefs. What do you truly believe about your potential? Your worth? Your abilities? You can't build a winning mindset on limiting beliefs. If your internal dialogue is filled with "I'm not good enough," or "I never finish what I start," then those beliefs will quietly sabotage everything you try to build. It's time to replace those beliefs with truth and power, because when you believe in your worth, your actions begin to match that belief.

Second, consistently check your attitude. Attitudes are the tone you set for your day. It's how you approach problems, setbacks, people, and tasks. Your mindset is the collection of those attitudes—added up over time. Start asking yourself: "Is my attitude toward this task helping me or hurting me?" "Is the way I think about this challenge moving me forward or pulling me back?" If the answer isn't aligned with your goal—shift it. Don't wait. Your goals should never be delayed.

Take consistent, aligned action. A powerful mindset isn't built in a single day—it's built by doing small things consistently with the right attitude. When you approach your work with excellence, your relationships with empathy, your growth with hunger—you create a mindset of strength. And that mindset becomes your edge. Your anchor. Your competitive advantage. Here's the bottom line: Your mindset isn't just what you think—it's what you allow yourself to think. It's not just what you feel—it's what you choose to feel. It's not just how you act—it's how you decide to show up, every single day. And when your mindset is aligned—when your attitudes are in harmony with your goals—you become an unstoppable force.

So don't just set goals, develop mental toughness. Choose attitudes that support your dreams, not sabotage them. Think thoughts that fuel your fire, not feed your fear. Align your whole being with who you want to be and where you want to go—and then press forward with everything you've got. When your mindset is right, nothing is out of reach.

Taking Action

Think | Write | Grow

Based on what you learned in this chapter:

What's something you will stop doing or a habit you will break?

_____

_____

What's something you will start doing or a habit you will create?

_____

_____

What's the potential positive impact of improving in this area?

_____

_____

Chapter Forty-Eight

Emotional Intelligence Is as Valuable as IQ

Rival 7: Mindset

F or years, we were told that IQ—the intelligence quotient—was the key to success. The smarter you were on paper, the better your test scores, the higher your grades, the brighter your future. However, research now confirms that emotional intelligence (EI) is just as valuable as IQ. Why? Because IQ can help you pass a test, but EQ can help you pass in life where it matters most.

Emotional intelligence is your ability to understand your own emotions, manage them effectively, recognize what's going on with others, and respond with empathy and the appropriate social skills, such as active listening. It's the secret skill behind strong leadership, healthy relationships, and lasting success. And the best part? Unlike IQ which begins to stabilize at adulthood, EQ can be developed, improved, and mastered at any stage of life.

Let me be clear—intelligence is a great gift and asset to possess and should not be undervalued. However, intelligence without a balance of soft skills can lead to social awkwardness, the absence of quality relationships, and the list goes on. Have you ever known someone who was incredibly smart but couldn't hold a meaningful and mutual conversation? Or someone with great technical skills but couldn't handle pressure, take feedback, or work collaboratively with a team? That's the difference EQ makes. Life is not just a logic puzzle that needs to be solved. It's a human experience, and your ability to navigate emotions—both yours and others'—determines how far you can go both personally and professionally.

The five pillars of emotional intelligence are self-awareness, self-regulation, empathy, self-motivation, and social skills. Self-awareness is knowing what you are feeling and why. Self-regulation is the ability to manage your emotions, regardless of the circumstances. Empathy is to metaphorically step into someone's shoes and to understand what they feel. Self-motivation is just that—the ability to motivate from within—with no need for a carrot or a stick. Last, social skills are the ability to listen and communicate effectively with various groups and personality types.

Let's face it—most of life's challenges are emotional, not intellectual. When your plans fall apart, it's your emotional intelligence that helps you stay focused. When someone criticizes you unfairly, it's EI that keeps you calm instead of becoming defensive. When you're leading others, it's your ability to listen, connect, and motivate that makes the difference—not your mathematical aptitude. And in a world full of uncertainty, high stress, and constant change, emotional intelligence isn't just helpful—it's essential.

Think of the most successful people you admire—not just in terms of fame or money, but in terms of character, integrity, and impact. What sets them apart? It's probably not "how smart they are" but, instead, how they handle pressure, treat others, actively listen with empathy, and stay positive and motivated. That's emotional intelligence at work.

The good news is, you can improve your EI every day. Start by checking in with yourself. Ask, "What am I feeling right now, and why?" Practice active listening. Let people feel heard before you respond. Give yourself permission to pause, breathe, and reflect. And when things go wrong—as they will—choose patiently responding instead of quickly reacting. In the end, emotional intelligence is the difference between knowing the path and being able to walk it with grace, strength, and purpose. Don't just train your mind—train your heart and emotions, because when EI leads, everything else follows.

Taking Action

Think | Write | Grow

Based on what you learned in this chapter:

What's something you will stop doing or a habit you will break?

_____

_____

What's something you will start doing or a habit you will create?

_____

_____

What's the potential positive impact of improving in this area?

_____

_____

Chapter Forty-Nine

Self-Actualization Is the Ultimate Goal

Rival 7: Mindset

There is a question we all ask ourselves at some point in life: What is this all for? What is the point of the long hours, the hard work, the sacrifice, the struggle? According to Abraham Maslow, the renowned psychologist, the answer is simple but powerful; self-actualization. Maslow believed that self-actualization is the highest level of human fulfillment and should be one of the ultimate goals in life. It's the place where your potential becomes your reality. Where who you are is aligned with who you were always meant to be. It's far more than just a fancy psychological term—it's about living a life that's filled with purpose and is in sync with your values, passions, and talents. When you have achieved self-actualization, you don't wake up to survive—you wake up to thrive.

Self-actualization is not about perfection—it's about progress with purpose. It's about breaking free from the expectations of others and listening to the quiet voice within you that says, "This is who I really am." It's the moment when you stop chasing applause and start pursuing a deeper meaning. When you stop climbing someone else's ladder and start building your own. When you stop living on autopilot and start living on fire. But the truth of the matter is that self-actualization doesn't happen by accident—it takes self-awareness, discipline, confidence, and courage.

To become everything you are capable of becoming, you must first let go of everything that's holding you back. The fear. The doubt. The false identities. The pressure to fit in. You have to get honest about who you are and who you want to become. And most of all—you have to stop settling for a life of mediocrity in the comfort zone. Many people stop at the lower levels of fulfillment. They settle for a life of security, comfort, or approval. And while those things matter, they are not the summit—not even close. They are stepping stones to the ultimate goal that motivates us.

The climb to self-actualization is steep. But the view from the top? Unmatched. Because when you reach that level—when you are living your truth, using your gifts, and fulfilling your unique purpose—you don't just live a successful life... you live a life of significance. You become a light for others. You become a force of inspiration. You become a leader—not by title, but by example. It's important to remember that self-actualization is not a destination—it's a journey. You don't wake up one day and say, "I've made it." You evolve into it daily by aligning your thoughts and actions with your authentic self.

Every time you choose growth over comfort, you take a step toward it. Every time you express your truth, honor your values, and give your best—you get closer. And every time you lift someone else up, simply by being fully you, you inspire them to do the same. So, how do you start? By identifying what lights you up. By being honest about what you've been avoiding and what parts of your past you need to face, once and for all. By declaring what the highest version of yourself looks like and taking steps toward that "perceived-self" today. You start by saying yes to the inner calling that keeps nudging you forward and by recognizing that you are worthy—not one day, but right now—of becoming everything you are meant to be.

Self-actualization is not reserved for the few. It is available to all of us—if we are willing to look within, rise above, and keep going. So here, I challenge you: don't just live—become. Become the person who likes what they see when they look in the mirror. Become the person who turns potential into purpose. Become the person who doesn't just exist—but shines. Because that's the real goal. That's the real win. That's self-actualization. It's one of your greatest callings, and it's yours for the taking!

Taking Action

Think | Write | Grow

Based on what you learned in this chapter:

What's something you will stop doing or a habit you will break?

_____

_____

What's something you will start doing or a habit you will create?

_____

_____

What's the potential positive impact of improving in this area?

_____

_____

Chapter Fifty

Summary of 7 Rivals

Conclusion

W e all carry invisible weights—silent forces that sabotage progress and hold our best selves hostage. They show up in many forms, such as the fear that keeps us frozen and the doubt that whispers "you can't" Or, like the memories of past failures that loop like broken records and the comfort of idleness that slowly dulls our edge. Throw in adversity that shakes our confidence and distractions that steal our focus, and it's no wonder our dreams often feel distant. But here's the truth: every obstacle we face—external or internal—can be overcome. The key lies in mastering our mindset.

Fear: The Illusion That Feels Real

Fear is a primal emotion. It exists to protect us—but in the modern world, it often does more harm than good. Fear of failure. Fear of rejection. Fear of not being enough. These aren't lions chasing us in the wild—they're our thoughts and the stories we tell ourselves. And, like any story, they can be rewritten. To overcome fear, you must confront it head-on. Action is the antidote. When you take even the smallest step toward what scares you, you prove to yourself that fear doesn't define you. Over time, courage grows. Confidence builds. And fear, once a giant, shrinks into the background noise it truly is.

Doubt: The Voice That Questions Everything

Doubt creeps in when you're on the edge of something great. It sounds rational, even protective, when it asks, "Are you sure you're ready?" But doubt is not a voice of reason—it's a defense mechanism rooted in insecurity. Overcoming doubt requires evidence. Look at your past wins, your resilience, your growth. Remind yourself of your preparation, your work ethic, your vision. When you doubt yourself, choose to believe in the version of you that showed up when it counted. Faith in yourself must be louder than the fear of what might go wrong.

The Past: A Place of Reference, Not Residence

Your past may explain you, but it does not define you. Too many people live chained to yesterday's mistakes, failures, and pain. But the past is not a prison—it's a classroom. Learn from it. Then move forward. Forgiveness—of yourself and others—is essential. Growth demands that you release what no longer serves you. Your future is too important to be held hostage by what's behind you. Look ahead. You're not who you were. You're who you choose to become.

Idleness: The Comfortable Trap

Comfort is the enemy of progress. Idleness feels good in the moment, but leaves you restless over time. Goals are not achieved through inspiration alone—they require discipline, action, and consistency. Break the cycle of idleness by setting clear intentions and taking daily steps, no matter how small. Momentum is built one decision at a time. Don't wait for motivation to show up. Show up first—and motivation will follow.

Adversity: The Furnace That Forges You

Every challenge you face is a chance to grow stronger. Adversity doesn't break you—it reveals you. It tests your character, sharpens your focus, and builds your endurance. Embrace the struggle. Let it refine you, not define you. The most resilient people aren't the ones who had it easy—they're the ones who faced hardship and kept going, regardless. Adversity is not the end of the road. Often, it's the beginning of your rise.

Distractions: The Thieves of Purpose

We live in a world of noise—notifications, temptations, endless scrolling. Distractions pull you away from your path, little by little. Overcoming them starts with awareness. Ask yourself: What's stealing my attention? What matters most right now? Build boundaries. Create space for deep focus. When you protect your time, you protect your potential.

Mindset: The Master Key

At the heart of it all is your mindset. Your thoughts shape your reality. A fixed mindset sees obstacles as dead ends. A growth mindset sees them as opportunities. Choose the latter. Train your mind to see beyond fear, doubt, and struggle. Speak life over your journey. Believe in the process. Stay consistent. And remember—progress isn't about perfection—it's about persistence.

Final Thoughts: Success Lives Within You

You don't need to be fearless, flawless, or always fired up. You just need to be willing—to rise above fear, to silence doubt, to leave the past behind, to fight through comfort, to grow from adversity, and to remain focused through the noise. You already have what it takes. The power to overcome and to succeed lives within you. Now prove it—one day, one step, one choice at a time.

www.ingramcontent.com/pod-product-compliance
Lightning Source LLC
Chambersburg PA
CBHW051515120626
46551CB00012B/931